TAKING A STAND
for the BIBLE

JOHN ANKERBERG
DILLON BURROUGHS

HARVEST HOUSE PUBLISHERS

EUGENE, OREGON

This book includes material based on or revised from select excerpts from *Handbook of Biblical Evidences, Why You Can Believe the Bible, Knowing the Truth About the Reliability of the Bible, The Facts on the King James Only Debate,* and *Fast Facts on Defending Your Faith,* all by John Ankerberg and John Weldon.

TAKING A STAND FOR THE BIBLE
Copyright © 2009 by John Ankerberg and Dillon Burroughs
Published by Harvest House Publishers
Eugene, Oregon 97402
www.harvesthousepublishers.com

Library of Congress Cataloging-in-Publication Data

Ankerberg, John, 1945-
   Taking a stand for the Bible / John Ankerberg and Dillon Burroughs.
     p. cm.
   ISBN 978-0-7369-2400-9 (pbk.)
   1. Bible—Evidences, authority, etc. I. Burroughs, Dillon. II. Title.
   BS480.A69 2009
   220.1—dc22

                                          2008036845

CONTENTS

Part Three: What Is *in* the Bible?

Appendixes

INTRODUCTION

The Bible is the world's best-selling and most influential book. Abraham Lincoln called it "the best gift God has given to man." Patrick Henry said, "It is worth all other books which were ever printed." Noted British statesman William Gladstone wrote that "an immeasurable distance separates it from all competitors" while the famous philosopher Immanuel Kant declared, "The Bible is the greatest benefit which the human race has ever experienced." A.M. Sullivan observed, "The cynic who ignores, ridicules, or denies the Bible, spurning its spiritual rewards and aesthetic excitement, contributes to his own moral anemia."[1]

But why should we honor the Bible? Because of the Bible's *impact*. Humans share a universal desire to seek God, because apart from God life ultimately lacks lasting meaning and purpose. In response, the Bible claims to be the revealed Word of God (John 1:12-13; 1 John 5:9-15). Its words communicate how we can have a personal relationship with God (John 3:16; 17:3). If the Bible's words are true, then in its pages we can find ultimate meaning for our lives and the God we seek. We can read of his supernatural and loving actions among people and nations in the Old Testament. We can experience his love and redemption through Jesus Christ in the New Testament.

However, many people do not believe there is one true God, and they deny that God has personally revealed himself through the

Bible. Some of these arguments derive from the theories of skeptical scholarship, which has produced volumes of works attacking the perspective that the Bible provides an accurate account of God's intervention and plans for human history. Yet even the most devout skeptics cannot deny the Bible's influence in history and its impact upon millions of lives around the globe.

The topics addressed in *Taking a Stand for the Bible* are vital because if solid evidence exists that the Bible is composed of accurately revealed words from God, its critics are promoting inaccurate information. If the Bible's words are true, such skeptics ultimately mislead those who listen to them. If the Bible alone is divine revelation, then by definition it is the most important book in the world, and it deserves to be recognized as what it claims to be: the guidebook for our lives on all matters of faith.

To take a stand for the Bible means we believe that all of what the Bible teaches is reliable. Its core message teaches that the one true God sent his only Son Jesus to die for our sins so men and women could inherit eternal life as a free gift by simply placing their faith in Christ and becoming one of his followers (John 3:16; Romans 3:22-26). Such a claim is phenomenal in its uniqueness and compassion. If skeptics are given only one reason to objectively examine the claims of the Bible, this alone should be sufficient, because if these claims are true, then God freely offers us more than we could ever imagine.

If the Bible is truly God's Word to us, and if we reject its message of salvation, then no other personal decision we make will be more consequential. None of us can ignore the issue of the reliability of the Bible—not merely its historical reliability but the answer to the question, What if it *is* true?

Our goal is that those who already follow Christ will be encouraged in their faith and that the undecided will be challenged to investigate the Bible more deeply—to read it, reflect upon its message, and ultimately to accept its claims. We share the desire of the apostle Paul, who wrote, "We…thank God continually because, when you received the word of God, which you heard from us, you accepted it not as the word of men, but as it actually is, the word of God, which is at work in you who believe" (1 Thessalonians 2:13).

Join in the journey of a lifetime that will impact your life today—and your eternity—as we share together in *Taking a Stand for the Bible!*

PART ONE:

How Did We Get the Bible?

1

The Uniqueness of the Bible:
What Makes It So Special?

Is the Bible really the most unique book in the world? What makes it special among all other writings throughout history? The facts of the Bible cannot be explained solely by human theories concerning its origin. The Bible itself claims that it is unique among all books and is God's Word to humanity. The God of Scripture has revealed himself as a God of truth, so errors in the original manuscripts of the Bible's books would prove that God was not their author.

In fact, some would argue that because no other religion offers genuine evidence for belief in their deity or gods, apart from the Bible we are forced to remain agnostic about God. He might exist, but beyond hints of God based on the complexity of the universe around us, we would know little about who God is. In this chapter, we'll discuss seven key concepts for understanding what sets the Bible apart as unique from other books or spiritual writings throughout history.

1. The Bible Claims to Be Inspired by God

The Bible claims to be the inspired Word of God. We may argue that it is not, but first we must come to grips with the fact that it claims this for itself. When we speak, our words can be said to be the product of our breath. In the Bible, the words from God are said to be God-breathed. The apostle Paul wrote that "all Scripture is God-breathed [Greek, *theopneustos*] and is useful for teaching, rebuking, correcting and training in righteousness, so that the man of God may be thoroughly equipped for every good work" (2 Timothy 3:16-17).

The theologian Benjamin Warfield made this observation about these verses:

> The Greek term has, however, nothing to say of inspiring or of inspiration: it speaks only of a "spiring" or "spira-tion." What it says of Scripture is, not that it is "breathed into by God" or is the product of the Divine "inbreathing" into its human authors, but that it is breathed out by God, "God-breathed," the product of the creative breath of God. In a word, what is declared by this fundamental passage is simply that the Scriptures are a Divine product, without any indication of how God has operated in producing them. No term could have been chosen, however, which would have more emphatically asserted the Divine production of Scripture than that which is here employed.[1]

What is the meaning of biblical inspiration? Biblical inspira-tion is...

- *Verbal:* extending to the very words, not just the ideas, of Scripture.

  > Jesus answered, "It is written: 'Man does not live on bread alone, but on every word that comes from the mouth of God'" (Matthew 4:4).

- *Plenary:* extending equally to every part of Scripture.

  > "I tell you the truth, until heaven and earth dis-appear, not the smallest letter, not the least stroke of a pen, will by any means disappear from the Law until everything is accomplished" (Matthew 5:18).

- *Clear:* sometimes called "perspicuous," meaning sufficiently clear for the average person to understand without scholarly or technical training.

> "The statutes of the LORD are trustworthy, making wise the simple" (Psalm 19:7).

Directly or indirectly, the Bible claims or implies divine inspiration on numerous occasions. Here are several examples:

> This word came to Jeremiah from the LORD: "Take a scroll and write on it all the words I have spoken to you concerning Israel, Judah and all the other nations from the time I began speaking to you in the reign of Josiah till now" (Jeremiah 36:1-2).

> Prophecy never had its origin in the will of man, but men spoke from God as they were carried along by the Holy Spirit (2 Peter 1:21).

> I did not speak of my own accord, but the Father who sent me commanded me what to say and how to say it… whatever I say is just what the Father has told me to say (John 12:49-50).

> The revelation of Jesus Christ, which God gave him to show his servants what must soon take place (Revelation 1:1).

In addition, we find an abundance of references throughout the Bible that prophets spoke "the word of the LORD." For example:

> In the past God spoke to our forefathers through the prophets at many times and in various ways (Hebrews 1:1).

> The word of the LORD that came to Hosea…(Hosea 1:1).

> The word of the LORD came to Ezekiel…(Ezekiel 1:3).

> Moses then wrote down everything the LORD had said (Exodus 24:4; see also 31:24).

> …you should remember the words spoken beforehand by

the holy prophets and the commandment of the Lord and Savior spoken by your apostles…[Our] beloved brother Paul, according to the wisdom given him, wrote to you… letters, speaking in them of these things, in which are some things hard to understand, which the untaught and unstable distort, as they do the rest of the Scriptures (2 Peter 3:2,15-16 NASB).

From these and many other similar references found throughout the Bible, we can clearly illustrate that the Bible repeatedly claims to be inspired from God. This alone does not prove that its words are inspired, but it does reveal what the Bible claims for itself.

2. The Bible Is Powerful

The Old Testament prophet Jeremiah quoted these words from God: "'Is not my word like fire,' declares the LORD, 'And like a hammer that breaks a rock in pieces?'" (Jeremiah 23:29). If the Bible is the Word of God, it is the most important work of literature on the planet. It is important for both what it says and what it does. Other statements in Scripture echo this same principle:

[God said] "My word that goes out from my mouth…will not return to me empty, but will accomplish what I desire and achieve the purpose for which I sent it" (Isaiah 55:11).

The word of God is living and active. Sharper than any double-edged sword, it penetrates even to dividing soul and spirit, joints and marrow; it judges the thoughts and attitudes of the heart (Hebrews 4:12).

Because of the Bible's divine nature, ignorance of it can have a spiritually negative impact on our lives. Its information divinely strengthens our lives; likewise, being unaware of its information weakens our lives. As Jesus told the hypocritical religious leaders of his day, "You are in error because you do not know the Scriptures or the power of God" (Matthew 22:29).

Interesting Facts about the Bible

The Bible is the world's best-selling and most translated book, but what is it?

Books in the Bible: 66
Books in the Old Testament: 39
Books in the New Testament: 27
Shortest book in the Bible: .... 2 John
Longest book in the Bible: .... Psalms
Chapters in the Bible: 1189
Chapters in the Old Testament: 929
Chapters in the New Testament: 260
Middle chapter of the Bible: .... Psalm 117
Shortest chapter in the Bible: .... Psalm 117
Longest chapter in the Bible: .... Psalm 119
Verses in the Bible: 31,173
Verses in the Old Testament: 23,214
Verses in the New Testament: 7,959
Shortest verse in the Bible: .... John 11:35
Longest verse in the Bible: .... Esther 8:9
Words in the Bible: 773,692
Words in the Old Testament: 592,439
Words in the New Testament: .... 181,253[2]

3. The Bible Communicates Its Own Authority

In multiple places and a myriad of ways, the pages of the Bible communicate it is a book of authority for all to follow. We can observe this pattern clearly throughout the Old Testament, the Gospels, and the rest of the New Testament.

The Old Testament

The Old Testament, covering the period from the creation of humanity to the 400s B.C., offers a consistent and strong stance that its words are revelation from God.

Eternal—These words will stand forever

- Isaiah 40:8: "The grass withers and the flowers fall, but the word of our God stands forever."
- Psalm 119:89: "Your word, O LORD, is eternal; it stands firm in the heavens."
- Psalm 138:2: "I will bow down toward your holy temple and will praise your name for your love and your faithfulness, for you have exalted above all things your name and your word."

Perfect and Trustworthy—These words will be tested

- Proverbs 30:5-6: "Every word of God is flawless; he is a shield to those who take refuge in him. Do not add to his words, or he will rebuke you and prove you a liar."
- Psalm 12:6: "The words of the LORD are flawless, like silver refined in a furnace of clay, purified seven times."
- Psalm 18:30: "As for God, his way is perfect; the word of the LORD is flawless. He is a shield for all who take refuge in him."
- Psalm 19:7,9: "The law of the LORD is perfect, reviving the soul…the ordinances of the LORD are sure and altogether righteous."

True—These words are true words

- Psalm 119:43,142,151,160: "The word of truth…your law is true…all your commandments are true…All your words are true; all your righteous laws are eternal."

Holy and Righteous—These words have been
set apart for God's use

- Psalm 105:42: "He remembered his holy promise given to his servant Abraham."

- Psalm 119:123: "My eyes fail, looking for your salvation, looking for your righteous promise."
- Psalm 119:140: "Your promises have been thoroughly tested, and your servant loves them."

Good—These words can bring God's goodness to our lives

- Jeremiah 33:14: "I will fulfill the gracious promise I made…"

Vital—These words bring people into a vital relationship with God

- Isaiah 59:21: " 'As for me, this is my covenant with them,' says the LORD. 'My Spirit, who is on you, and my words that I have put in your mouth will not depart from your mouth, or from the mouths of your children, or from the mouths of their descendants from this time on and forever,' says the LORD."

Jesus Christ and the Gospels

Jesus, who claimed to be the Son of God, added his authority to the words of the Bible as well:

Eternal—Jesus' words will never pass away

- Matthew 24:35: "Heaven and earth will pass away, but my words will never pass away."

Trustworthy—Jesus taught that you can believe the Bible is God's Word

- Matthew 5:18: "I tell you the truth, until heaven and earth disappear, not the smallest letter, not the least stroke of a pen, will by any means disappear from the Law until everything is accomplished."

- John 5:47: "Since you do not believe what he [Moses] wrote, how are you going to believe what I say?"
- John 10:35: "...the Scripture cannot be broken."
- John 12:49-50: "I did not speak of my own accord, but the Father who sent me commanded me what to say and how to say it. I know that his command leads to eternal life. So whatever I say is just what the Father has told me to say."
- John 17:8: "I gave them the words you gave me..."
- Luke 16:17: "It is easier for heaven and earth to disappear than for the least stroke of a pen to drop out of the Law."

True—Jesus taught the truths of the Bible will purify your life

- John 17:17: "Sanctify them by the truth; your word is truth."

Holy—Jesus said His teaching was God's teaching

- John 7:16: "My teaching is not my own. It comes from him who sent me."

Vital—Jesus said to follow Scripture if you truly want to live

- Matthew 4:4: "Jesus answered, 'It is written: "Man does not live on bread alone, but on every word that comes from the mouth of God." ' "

The Rest of the New Testament

It is important to note that Jesus' followers held a consistent view with the words spoken by Jesus in the Gospels. They, too, considered the Old Testament God's Word, in addition to the writings of the apostles:

Eternal—God's Word will last for eternity
- 1 Peter 1:25: "The word of the Lord stands forever. And this is the word that was preached to you."

Inspired—The Bible is an extension of God himself
- 2 Timothy 3:16-17: "All Scripture is God-breathed and is useful for teaching, rebuking, correcting and training in righteousness, so that the man of God may be thoroughly equipped for every good work."
- 2 Peter 1:20-21: "...no prophecy of Scripture came about by the prophet's own interpretation. For prophecy never had its origin in the will of man, but men spoke from God as they were carried along by the Holy Spirit."
- 2 Peter 3:2,15-16: "I want you to recall the words spoken in the past by the holy prophets and the command given by our Lord and Savior through your apostles...Bear in mind that our Lord's patience means salvation, just as our dear brother Paul also wrote you with the wisdom that God gave him. He writes the same way in all his letters, speaking in them of these matters. His letters contain some things that are hard to understand, which ignorant and unstable people distort, as they do the other Scriptures, to their own destruction." (This passage shows the inspiration of the New Testament.)

Living and Active—The Bible is powerful for our lives
- Hebrews 4:12: "The word of God is living and active..."
- 1 Peter 1:23: "You have been born again, not of perishable seed, but of imperishable, through the living and enduring word of God."

True—The Bible provides accurate information concerning key areas of life

- 2 Timothy 2:15: "Do your best to present yourself to God as one approved, a workman who does not need to be ashamed and who correctly handles the word of truth."

Supernatural—The Bible is divine in its origin

- 1 Thessalonians 2:13: "We also thank God continually because, when you received the word of God, which you heard from us, you accepted it not as the word of men, but as it actually is, the word of God, which is at work in you who believe."

- 1 Thessalonians 4:8: "…he who rejects this instruction does not reject man but God, who gives you his Holy Spirit."

Holy—God's Word is set apart as special from all other writings

- 2 Timothy 3:15: "…from infancy you have known the holy Scriptures."

Vital—The Bible is essential to our lives

- Revelation 22:18-19: "I warn everyone who hears the words of the prophecy of this book: If anyone adds anything to them, God will add to him the plagues described in this book. And if anyone takes words away from this book of prophecy, God will take away from him his share in the tree of life and in the holy city, which are described in this book."

- 1 Corinthians 2:12-13: "We have not received the spirit of the world but the Spirit who is from God, that we may understand what God has freely given us…in words taught by the Spirit."

- Romans 3:2: "…they have been entrusted with the very words [Greek: *logia*] of God."

The Character of God and the Inerrancy of Scripture

- Sovereign: A sovereign God is able to preserve the process of inspiration from error.
- Righteousness: A righteous God would never inspire error.
- Just: A just God could not lie when asserting that his word is perfect or without error. He would be unjust if he called error-filled Scripture "holy and true."
- Love: A loving God would adequately provide for the spiritual health and safety of his people by inspiring Scripture.
- Eternal: An eternal God has had eternity to plan for his perfect word.
- Omniscient: An all-knowing God knows every contingency that might arise to make his words flawed.
- Omnipotent: An all-powerful God can effectively respond to every contingency and also preserve the transmission of his Word.
- Omnipresent: A God who is everywhere at all times can reveal and inspire his word because all factors are within his sight and control.
- Truthful: A truthful God would not lie when he speaks concerning his words.
- Merciful: A merciful God would not trick people by stating his word is perfect if it is not.
- Personal: A personal God can inspire verbally, the words he gives, to ensure effective communication.

4. The Bible Is Unique in Its Teachings and Details

No other book in history compares to the unique combination of spiritual teachings and details of accuracy as provided in the Bible. For instance:

- The Bible is the only book that offers objective evidence to be the Word of God, offering real proof of its divine inspiration.

- The Bible is the only religious Scripture in the world that can logically be considered without errors in its original copies.

- The Bible is the only ancient book with documented scientific and medical prevision. In fact, many modern books have been written on the theme of the Bible and modern science.

- The Bible is the only religious Scripture that offers eternal salvation as a free gift entirely by God's grace and mercy.

- The Bible is the only ancient religious Scripture whose complete text has been preserved with such an extreme level of accuracy.

- Only the Bible describes the creation of the universe by God from outside space and time and then gives a continuous historical record from the first man, Adam, to the end of history.

- Only the Bible contains detailed prophecies about the coming Savior of the world and whose prophecies have proven true in history.

- Only the Bible has unique theological content that includes the Trinity (that God is Father, Son, and Holy Spirit), the sinful nature of humanity, and the physical resurrection of Jesus from death.

- Only the Bible offers a realistic and permanent remedy for the problem of human sin and evil.

- Only the Bible has its accuracy confirmed in history, archaeology, and other sciences.

- The internal and historical characteristics of the Bible are unique in its unity and internal consistency despite production over a 1500-year period by 40-plus authors in three languages on three continents discussing scores of controversial subjects yet having agreement on all issues.

- The Bible is the most translated, purchased, and persecuted book in history.

- Only the Bible is fully one-quarter prophetic, containing a total of some 400 complete pages of predictions.

- Only the Bible has withstood 2000 years of intense scrutiny by critics, not only surviving the attacks but prospering and having its credibility strengthened by such criticism.

- The Bible has molded the history of Western civilization more than any other book and achieved worldwide influence.

- Only the Bible has a person-specific (Christ-centered) focus for each of its 66 books, detailing Christ's life in prophecy 400-1500 years before his birth on earth.

- Only the Bible proclaims a resurrection of its central figure that is proven in history.

5. The Bible Is Unique in Its Straightforward Interpretation

The Bible declares that it is our responsibility to interpret the Bible accurately. The apostle Paul wrote to Timothy, "Do your best to present yourself to God as one approved, a workman who does not need to be ashamed and who correctly handles the word of truth" (2 Timothy 2:15). The reason that members of alternative religious movements misinterpret the Bible is often because they have not studied or properly applied the principles for correctly interpreting a historical document like the Bible. John Ankerberg and John Weldon's reference work *Encyclopedia of Cults and New Religions* documents numerous examples of how cults and other religious groups misinterpret the Bible by failing to adhere to accepted rules of textual interpretation for literature.[3]

In order to approach the Word of God correctly, we must become familiar with the basic principles of interpretation, such as that the Bible is generally to be interpreted normally or literally. There is no justification for coming to the text to interpret all of its words mystically or symbolically, or through the alleged insights of so-called higher consciousness or alleged new divine revelations that contradict the Bible's earlier revelation. To interpret the Bible normally means attention must be paid to what the authors *originally intended,* what the words they wrote meant to them in their linguistic and historical context. The point is to discover the writer's intent. This meaning is fixed by the author and is not open to our own personal interpretations or bias. Our goal must be to understand the text in its context before we seek to apply its meaning to our lives today.

Bible verses can often be better understood with reference to the original languages of Scripture—Greek, Hebrew, and Aramaic—including word meanings and grammar. Comparing similar or parallel passages relevant to the particular verse or topic is also important. Bible verses must be interpreted both in their immediate and larger context. This may require some understanding of the author, and the general historical context, such as the time period in which the particular Bible book was written. Just as it would not be wise to interpret a single sentence in a magazine article by itself, but in the context of the entire article, we would also be wise to interpret verses from the Bible within their larger contexts.

Understanding the literary genre of a passage is also important. For example, we interpret the parables of Jesus in a different way than we do the historical accounts in the book of Acts. In addition, because the Bible is a compilation of progressive revelation (meaning more information is revealed over time), the Old Testament sometimes needs to be text-interpreted based on later teachings in the New Testament. Another helpful principle is to interpret unclear portions of the Bible with help from clearer portions. That's because the Bible's teachings, if perfect, must be consistent with one another.

If we respect the Bible as the Word of God, apply proper interpretive principles, and depend upon the Holy Spirit to help us interpret and apply it properly, our reverent study will bring great rewards. It will also astonish us how the message of the Bible is consistent with itself from beginning to end.

6. Jesus' View of the Bible

Some religious groups argue that the Bible has become corrupted during the history of the church or claim to have received new revelations that correct or complete the Bible. But what such groups ultimately fail to do is to honor the words of Jesus, whom they claim to revere.

Jesus said plainly, without any reservations, that, "Your word is truth" (John 17:17). He said that heaven and earth would pass away but that his words would never pass away (Matthew 24:35). In John 14:26 he promised the disciples that the Holy Spirit would teach them all things and bring to remembrance the things Jesus had taught them. He taught that the Holy Spirit, whom he would send, would guide the disciples into all truth (John 16:13). By doing so, he alluded to the inspiration and inerrancy of the New Testament before it was even written.

Clearly, Jesus did not believe that the Holy Spirit, whom he called "the Spirit of truth" (John 14:17), would corrupt his own words or inspire error. As the Son of God, Jesus was a perfect and reliable authority. As the only person in history to resurrect himself from the dead (John 2:19), his view of Scripture holds precedence over what anyone else says.

7. The Bible Is Proven Reliable Historically

We will discuss this seventh point in greater detail in parts two and three of this book, but it is worth mentioning here that the Bible is unique based on its proven historical reliability. Archaeologists have discovered over 25,000 places or facts consistent with the historical locations and times cited in the Bible. Names of kings and queens and time lines of history, wars, and kingdoms have been proven consistent with biblical teachings time and time again, leading many skeptics to ultimately regard the Bible as a helpful resource in researching ancient history.

The Bible is not just one book; it is a 66-book anthology produced over multiple generations, yet reliable to the smallest detail. In our next chapter, we'll step beyond the uniqueness of the Bible to take a look at how the Bible's books were collected together into the one volume we enjoy today. As we do, we'll discover God's hand at work in both the writing of the Bible and in its continued compilation and translation from ancient scrolls to the digital world of our time.

2

THE INSPIRATION OF THE BIBLE:
How Can It Be God's Word?

Who wrote the Bible? Our answer to this question will not only determine how we view the Bible, but will also ultimately have an eternal impact on our lives. If the Bible is really God's Word, then we should honor, study, apply, and trust it. If the Bible is the Word of God, then to dismiss it is to dismiss the God who authored it.

The fact that God gave us the Bible is an evidence of his love for us. The term *revelation* simply means that God communicated to humanity what he is like and how we can have a right relationship with him. These are things that we could not have known had not God divinely revealed them to us in the Bible. Although God's revelation of himself was progressively revealed over a period of approximately 1500 years, it has always contained everything people have needed to know about God in order to have a right relationship with him. If the Bible is truly the Word of God, then it is the final authority for all matters of faith and spiritual practice.

That brings us to our next set of questions: How can we know that the Bible is the Word of God and not just a good book? What is unique about the Bible that sets it apart from all other religious books? We must answer these types of questions if we are to seriously examine the claim that the Bible is the very Word of God, divinely inspired, and completely sufficient for all issues of life.

The Bible Is Inspired by God

First, there can be no doubt that the Bible itself claims to be the very Word of God. This claim is clearly seen in 2 Timothy 3:15-17:

> ...from infancy you have known the holy Scriptures, which are able to make you wise for salvation through faith in Christ Jesus. *All Scripture* is *God-breathed* and is useful for teaching, rebuking, correcting and training in righteousness, so that the man of God may be thoroughly equipped for every good work (emphasis added).

Scripture is also called "God-breathed." This term is translated from a unique word in the Greek New Testament that literally means that the words are of God and therefore an extension of God himself. Thus when we learn God's Word, we can know God personally and be properly trained for the lifestyle God has designed for us.

Here are some implications we can draw from 2 Timothy 3:16:

1. Inspiration deals with the objective text of Scripture, not the subjective intention of the reader.

2. The doctrine of Scripture applies to *all* or *every* scripture—that is, the Bible in part or in whole is the Word of God.

3. The Scriptures *are* the very breathed-out Word of God. The *form and content* of Scripture are the very words of God. This does not mean that each individual word is inspired *as such* but only *as part of a whole* sentence or unit of meaning. There is no implication in Scripture of an *atomistic* inspiration of each word but only of a *holistic* inspiration of all words used. Just as an individual word has no meaning apart from its use in a given context, so individual words of Scripture are not inspired apart from their use in a whole sentence.[1]

Human and Divine

God makes it very clear in the Bible that he used both human and divine means to communicate revealed truth. In 2 Peter 1:20-21, we find that the prophets wrote as the Holy Spirit enabled them: "Above all, you must understand that no prophecy of Scripture came about by the prophet's own interpretation. For prophecy never had its origin in the will of man, but men spoke from God as they were carried along by the Holy Spirit." Further, we are told that the meaning of the words were not from the writer but rather from the ultimate author, God.

What process did God use to communicate his Word to us? First, God spoke to the prophets. This was done in many and various ways (Hebrews 1:1). These various ways included:

Ways God Spoke to the Prophets in the Old Testament

By angels	Genesis 18–19
In dreams	Daniel 7; Numbers 12:6
In visions	Isaiah 1:1; Ezekiel 1:1; 8:3; 11:24; Hosea 12:10
Through nature	Psalm 19:1
An audible voice	1 Samuel 3:4
Inner voice	Many times, using the formula "And the word of the LORD came to me…"
By Urim and Thummim	Exodus 28:30; Numbers 27:21
Casting lots	Proverbs 16:33
Through other prophetic writings	Daniel 9:1-2

God did not only speak in various ways; he spoke in the words of the prophets. To put it another way, the prophets' messages were God's messages (Jeremiah 1:9).

Our ultimate authority regarding whether the Bible is God-inspired Scripture or not comes directly from the teachings of Jesus. In Matthew 5:17, Jesus notes that he came not to end the law but rather to fulfill it. In the very next verse, he teaches that even the smallest letter of the law would not pass until all is accomplished. Later, in John 10:35, Jesus stated that Scripture cannot be broken, which means Jesus testified to the complete authority and reliability of Scripture.

In addition to the above, several times in the Bible we observe that God directly commanded others to write down his words. For example, in Exodus 17:4 Moses was instructed to have God's words recorded in writing. The same was true of the prophets, including Jeremiah (Jeremiah 30:2) and Isaiah (Isaiah 30:8).

In terms of practical application, we realize that: (1) God's Word is true, (2) the words in the Bible are God's truth, (3) learning and obeying this truth is vital to our spiritual maturity, and (4) the Bible's teachings provide our ultimate basis for living a life that honors God. The person who observes and practices the truth of God as found in the Bible will be the blessed man or woman God desires (Psalm 1).

What the Bible Says, God Says

Is the Bible really the Word of God, or is it nothing more than another collection of human words? If it is the Word of God, how can we know the information within its pages came from God? Some people say parts of the Bible came from God, but then claim there are also errors in it. In an interview with Dr. Norman Geisler, founder of Southern Evangelical Seminary and author of over 60 books, I (John) asked Dr. Geisler to answer the question, "Does it matter whether or not there are errors in the Bible?"

He responded by saying, "Is it dangerous to live downstream from a cracked dam? Ask the people in Toccoa Falls, Georgia. There's a little college nestled in the valley there near beautiful waterfalls. Years ago, an earthen dam existed behind the falls overlooking the campus. Over a period of time, a crack began to form in this dam. The Army Corps of Engineers assured people repeatedly that the dam was safe and that the crack was nothing to worry about. One night in 1977, the dam burst and the waters swept down the valley. Dozens of people were killed. The students and citizens of this quaint little college community have learned that it's dangerous to live downstream from a cracked dam."

You might be thinking, *What does this cracked dam illustration have to do with how the books of the Bible became one book?* There are people telling us there are errors in the Bible, just little, insignificant ones, just like the crack in the dam was once insignificant. Are there errors in the Bible, or is the Bible the inerrant Word of God?

Another way we know the Bible is God's Word is by how the Bible uses statements regarding what God said and what Scripture says. The following chart, discussed by Dr. Geisler in our interview, reveals that the Old Testament Scripture is clearly God's Word:

What the Bible Says...God Says (and Vice Versa)

God said	Scripture said
Genesis 12:3 "I will bless those who bless you, and whoever curses you I will curse; and all peoples on earth will be blessed through you."	Galatians 3:8 "The Scripture foresaw that God would justify the Gentiles by faith, and announced the gospel in advance to Abraham: 'All nations will be blessed through you.'"
Exodus 9:6	Romans 9:17

Bible said	God said
Genesis 2:24	Matthew 19:4-5
Psalm 95:7	Hebrews 3:7
Psalm 2:1	Acts 4:24-25
Isaiah 55:3	Acts 13:34
Psalm 16:10	Acts 13:35
Psalm 2:7	Hebrews 1:5
Psalm 97:7	Hebrews 1:6
Psalm 104:4	Hebrews 1:7

But what about the New Testament? Is it also the inspired Word of God? Many of the verses we just cited refer to the Old Testament because the New Testament wasn't written when Jesus made the statements he did. In 2 Peter 3:16, the apostle Peter places the apostle Paul's letters on the same level of authority as the inspired writings of the Old Testament. And the apostle Paul quotes a verse found in the Gospel of Luke as Scripture (1 Timothy 5:18).

The Word of God is inspired, and the New Testament is the Word of God. Hebrews 4:12 mentions that the Word of God is "living and active." Therefore, the New Testament is also living and active. It's not just the Old Testament that claims to be the Word of God, but every book in the New Testament claims to come from an apostle of God or those who were companions of the apostles (such as Mark and Luke). God's truth was revealed by Jesus (the incarnation of God himself, John 1:1-4), and as Hebrews 4:12 says, it is living and active. So the entire Bible, both the Old and New Testaments, can be trusted to be the Word of God.

Where Did We Get the Bible?

The Bible is unique among all the ancient books of the world. Forty authors were involved in writing this masterpiece over a period of 1500 years. One could expect errors and inaccuracies with any other book credited to so many authors and so much time involved in the writing of it. However, God's supernatural intervention produced a book without error and a collection of writings in agreement in its essentials. Only God, in his infinite wisdom and divine providence, could produce such a flawless work.

Let's discuss the New Testament for a moment. How were the 27 New Testament books made available to us? Everything starts with Jesus. Most scholars hold that Jesus taught from his late twenties to his early thirties. He chose 12 apostles and taught them for three years. Eleven of them went on to spread his message. The New Testament books were based on a connection with the apostles and the teachings of Jesus.

The 27 books have nine basic sources (highlighted in bold text below):

- Two apostles of Jesus, **Matthew** and **John**, wrote Gospels. John also wrote three letters and the book of Revelation. The apostle **Peter** authored two letters and was the source for **Mark**'s Gospel. Peter also recognized the apostle **Paul**'s writings as Scripture (2 Peter 3:16).

- **Luke** based his Gospel on the eyewitness testimony of the apostles (Luke 1:1-3). He was also a traveling companion of the apostle Paul. Paul later quotes Luke's Gospel as Scripture (1 Timothy 5:18).

- **James** and **Jude** were human half-brothers of Jesus. James did not believe in Christ until after the resurrection of Jesus when Jesus appeared to him. James later became bishop of the Jerusalem church and wrote the New Testament book bearing his name. Jude believed after the resurrection as well, writing the book that bears his name.

- **The author of Hebrews** was well known to his recipients but not to everyone in the church. This delayed its acceptance to some. Many claim the author was Barnabas, a fellow missionary with Paul. Others believe Apollos wrote it during his early years with Paul in Corinth. Others argue for Paul as the author. Regardless, the writer had direct contact with an apostle.

Nine individuals wrote the 27 books received by the churches and recognized as Scripture. All were written and received before A.D. 96. Within approximately one generation of the New Testament's completion, every book had been cited by an early church father. It was in A.D. 367 that Athanasius wrote an authoritative list of the 27 books accepted by all of Christendom.

How do we know that the books of the Bible we have today are accurate copies of what the New Testament authors actually wrote?

When researching the New Testament, we find that the number of the earliest manuscripts available far exceed the number of manuscripts available for any other work in history. The earliest fragments we have of the Gospel of John range from within one generation of the apostle John's life (approximately A.D. 125). So if John wrote something in A.D. 95, then the earliest copies we have available to us are a mere 30 years removed from the time the original text was written.

In total, over 5300 copies of the Greek texts (the original New Testament language), 10,000 copies of Latin texts, and 9300 copies of other versions, exist from the early church era. By comparison, of 16 well-known classical Greek authors, the typical number of early copies that still exist is *less than ten,* with the earliest copies dating from 750 to 1600 years *after* the originals were written. This means if you reject the accuracy of the New Testament, you would also have to reject all the other writings in ancient history because none of them have copies today that are a short time removed from the original texts. By contrast, the copies we have of the New Testament are much earlier, and we have more copies available.

Sir Frederick Kenyon, formerly director and principal librarian of the British Museum, once wrote concerning the Bible:

> In no other case is the interval of time between the composition of the book and the date of the earliest extant [existing] manuscripts so short as in that of the New Testament. The interval, then, between the dates of original composition and the earliest extant evidence [existing copies] become so small as to be in fact negligible, and the last foundation for any doubt that the Scriptures have come down to us substantially as they were written, has now been removed. Both the authenticity and the general integrity of the books of the New Testament may be regarded as finally established.[2]

Outside of the New Testament, several additional early writings connect with the events of historic Christianity. The second generation of Christianity includes eight clear sources supporting its authority. New Testament Greek scholar Dr. Kurt Aland comments that the New Testament "was not imposed from the top, be it by bishops or synods, and then accepted by the communities... The organized church did not create the canon [New Testament]; it recognized the canon that had been created."[3]

How Were the New Testament Books Selected?

But just how were the New Testament books selected? The basic historical rules that guided recognition of the canon are as follows, written in question format:

1. Was the book written or supported by a prophet or apostle of God?

This was the single most important factor. The reasoning here is that the Word of God, which is inspired by the Spirit of God for the people of God, must be communicated through a person of God. If an apostle cast out demons, healed the sick, and raised the dead, you would quickly recognize that you should listen to this person. Jesus' apostles were well known.

2. Is the book authoritative?

In other words, can it be said of the book as it was said of Jesus, "The people were amazed at his teaching, because he taught them as one who had authority, not as the teachers of the law" (Mark 1:22)? Put another way, does this book ring with the sense of "The Lord says..."?

3. Does the book tell the truth about God consistent with previous revelation?

The Bereans searched the Old Testament Scriptures to determine whether Paul's teaching was true (Acts 17:11). They knew that if Paul's teaching did not resonate with the Old Testament writings, it could not be of God. Agreement with all earlier revelation was essential (Galatians 1:8).

4. Does the book give evidence of having the power of God?

Any writing that does not exhibit the transforming power of God in the lives of its readers could not have come from God. Scripture says that the Word of God is "living and active" (Hebrews 4:12). So if the book in question did not have the power to change a life, then the book could not have come from God.

5. Was the book accepted by the people of God?

In Old Testament times, Moses' scrolls were immediately placed into the Ark of the Covenant (Deuteronomy 31:24-26), as were Joshua's (Joshua 24:26). In the New Testament, Paul thanked the Thessalonians for receiving his message as the Word of God (1 Thessalonians 2:13). Paul's letters were also circulated among the churches (Colossians 4:16; 1 Thessalonians 5:27). The majority of God's people initially accepted Scripture as God's Word.

But what about the Old Testament? Dr. Geisler presents the case about the facts of the Old Testament this way:

> Jesus taught definitely that God was the originator of the Hebrew Old Testament. He taught as authoritative or authentic most of the books of the Hebrew canon...he asserted that the Old Testament as a whole was unbreakable scripture (John 10:35); that it would never perish (Matthew 5:18); and that it must be fulfilled (Luke 24:44)...Jesus not only defined the limits...but he laid down the principle of canonicity.[4]

In Luke 24:44, Jesus categorized all the books of the Old Testament when he referred to the Law, the Prophets, and the Writings. These represented the three major classifications of the Hebrew Old Testament.

How do we know the Bible is God's Word? Because Jesus told us. He is the One who claimed to be God and proved his claim by rising from the dead. It is on his authority as God of the universe that we are sure the Bible is the Word of God. Jesus confirmed the

Old Testament's authority, as well as an authoritative New Testament through his disciples. Jesus affirmed the Old Testament to be the Word of God and promised to guide his disciples to know all truth. Jesus claimed for the Bible:

- Divine authority (Matthew 3:3,7,10)
- Indestructability (Matthew 5:17-18)
- Infallibility (John 10:35)
- Ultimate supremacy (Matthew 15:3,6)
- Factual inerrancy (Matthew 22:29; John 17:17)
- Historical reliability (Matthew 12:40, 24:37-38)
- Scientific accuracy (Matthew 19:4-5; John 3:12)[5]

If Jesus is God's Son, then on his authority we can affirm that the Bible is the Word of God.

At this point, skeptics would claim that we are arguing in a circle, using the authority of Jesus as God's Son as evidence that the Bible is God's Word. However, first we investigate the evidence found in the Gospels concerning Jesus to see if he is God's Son. For this investigation, we do not start with the idea that these books are inspired or inerrant. We simply ask, "Do they provide accurate historical information about Jesus?" If yes, then we can conclude Jesus is God and what he says about the Bible is authoritative (For a discussion about the historical evidence regarding Jesus, see our book *What's the Big Deal About Jesus?*).

How Do We Understand the Bible?

A proper understanding of the Bible can be found in two important concepts: illumination and inspiration. *Illumination* means that to understand God's Word, we must have God's Spirit living within us. Without the Spirit's help, we are limited in our understanding. Paul wrote in 1 Corinthians 2:14, "The man without the Spirit does not accept the things that come from the Spirit of God, for they are foolishness to him, and he cannot understand them, because they are spiritually discerned."

Jesus also promised us that those who know God will have the capability to understand his Word. In John 16:12-15, Jesus said:

> I have much more to say to you, more than you can now bear. But when he, the Spirit of truth, comes, he will guide you into all truth. He will not speak on his own; he will speak only what he hears, and he will tell you what is yet to come. He will bring glory to me by taking from what is mine and making it known to you. All that belongs to the Father is mine. That is why I said the Spirit will take from what is mine and make it known to you.

Here, we are shown that the Holy Spirit is our teacher (verse 13), that the Spirit speaks truth (verse 13), and that the purpose is to glorify Jesus (verse 14). Understanding God's Word is ultimately a way in which Christ is honored and glorified.

The other aspect is *interpretation*. While God offers believers an understanding of truth, this does not mean diligent study is unnecessary. On the contrary, because God's Word is literally "God-breathed," an extension of himself, a continuous encounter with Scripture is vital to a healthy spiritual walk.

Acts 17 tells us of people who studied Scripture in their effort to seek the truth. There, Paul, a well-known teacher, provides teaching to a group of people called the Bereans. When the Bereans heard Paul teach, they checked the Scriptures before accepting Paul's teaching as true. They were determined to understand for themselves what God had spoken.

However, the Bereans were far different from some Thessalonians mentioned in Acts 17:1-9. There we read the following:

> When they had passed through Amphipolis and Apollonia, they came to Thessalonica, where there was a Jewish synagogue. As his custom was, Paul went into the synagogue, and on three Sabbath days he reasoned with them from the

Scriptures, explaining and proving that the Christ had to suffer and rise from the dead. "This Jesus I am proclaiming to you is the Christ," he said. Some of the Jews were persuaded and joined Paul and Silas, as did a large number of God-fearing Greeks and not a few prominent women.

But the Jews were jealous; so they rounded up some bad characters from the marketplace, formed a mob and started a riot in the city. They rushed to Jason's house in search of Paul and Silas in order to bring them out to the crowd. But when they did not find them, they dragged Jason and some other brothers before the city officials, shouting: "These men who have caused trouble all over the world have now come here, and Jason has welcomed them into his house. They are all defying Caesar's decrees, saying that there is another king, one called Jesus." When they heard this, the crowd and the city officials were thrown into turmoil. Then they made Jason and the others post bond and let them go.

The jealous Jews in Thessalonica heard God's truth, yet *rejected* it. The Bereans, by contrast, *investigated* it.

In Mark 13:31, Jesus said, "Heaven and earth will pass away, but my words will never pass away." Why will his words never pass away? Because they are of God, and God is eternal. Yet the daily implications of these sacred words are often difficult for us to process today. We find ourselves asking, "How does this apply to me today?"

The Bible was written to reveal God's instructions for life. As Christians interact with it and study it, they find power for their daily lives from the God of eternity, who assures them he is with them now and they have a future with him in heaven. In some ways, the Bible serves as a lifeline between them and God. Jesus said it best when he responded to temptation with the words, "Man does not live on bread alone, but on every word that comes from the mouth of God" (Matthew 4:4).

If you could have a conversation with Jesus, what would you ask him? What do you want to know? In many ways, reading God's Word is like communicating directly with God himself and allowing him to speak to us. Psalm 19:7-14 provides the fitting closing words on this topic:

> The law of the LORD is perfect,
>   reviving the soul.
> The statutes of the LORD are trustworthy,
>   making wise the simple.
>
> The precepts of the LORD are right,
>   giving joy to the heart.
> The commands of the LORD are radiant,
>   giving light to the eyes.
>
> The fear of the LORD is pure,
>   enduring forever.
> The ordinances of the LORD are sure
>   and altogether righteous.
>
> They are more precious than gold,
>   than much pure gold;
> they are sweeter than honey,
>   than honey from the comb.
>
> By them is your servant warned;
>   in keeping them there is great reward.
>
> Who can discern his errors?
>   Forgive my hidden faults.
>
> Keep your servant also from willful sins;
>   may they not rule over me.
> Then will I be blameless,
>   innocent of great transgression.
>
> May the words of my mouth and the meditation of my heart
>   be pleasing in your sight,
>   O LORD, my Rock and my Redeemer.

THE REPRODUCTION OF THE BIBLE:
What Happened to Get the Bible from Then to Now?

To date, over 5700 Greek manuscripts comprising parts of or whole books from the New Testament have been found, dating from the earliest period of church history. In total, over 24,000 ancient citations exist. If we compare these figures to the number of early copies found for other ancient literature, we see that no other work of writing compares in quantity.

Following is a chart that depicts the number of New Testament manuscripts that have been found compared to other early writings, such as those of Plato and Euripides. We notice that the document that comes closest in terms of the time between the original writing and its earliest existing copy is Homer's *Iliad*, with 500 years separating the two. When we look at the materials from this perspective, the New Testament stands as the best-documented book in history. As the New Testament scholar F.F. Bruce (Manchester University, Rylands Professor of Biblical Criticism and Exegesis) said, "There is no body of ancient literature in the world which enjoys such a wealth of good textual attestation as the New Testament."[1]

Author[2]	Date Written	Earliest Copy	Approximate Time Span Between Original & Copy	Number of Copies
Pliny	A.D. 61–113	A.D. 850	750 years	7
Plato	427–347 B.C.	A.D. 900	1200 years	7
Demosthenes	4th cent. B.C.	A.D. 110	800 years	8
Herodotus	480–425 B.C.	A.D. 900	1300 years	8
Suetonius	A.D. 75–160	A.D. 950	800 years	8
Thucydides	460–400 B.C.	A.D. 900	1300 years	8
Euripides	480–406 B.C.	A.D. 1100	1300 years	9
Aristophanes	450–385 B.C.	A.D. 900	1200 years	10
Caesar	100–44 B.C.	A.D. 900	1000 years	10
Tacitus	circa A.D. 100	A.D. 1100	1000 years	20
Aristotle	384–322 B.C.	A.D. 1100	1400 years	49
Sophocles	496–406 B.C.	A.D. 1000	1400 years	193
Homer *(Iliad)*	900 B.C.	400 B.C.	500 years	643
New Testament	1st cent. A.D. A.D. 50–100	2nd cent. A.D. (c. A.D. 130 onward)	less than 100 years	5700

Can the Bible Be Flawed?

Critics claim the Bible is filled with errors. Some even speak of thousands of mistakes. By contrast, Christians through the ages have claimed that the Bible is without error in the original text. Who is correct?

The argument for an errorless (inerrant) Bible can be put in this logical form:

1. God cannot be wrong.

2. The Bible is the Word of God.

3. Therefore, the Bible cannot be wrong.

An infinitely perfect, all-knowing God cannot make a mistake. The Scriptures testify to this, declaring emphatically that "it is impossible for God to lie" (Hebrews 6:18).

According to Jesus, "Until heaven and earth disappear, not the smallest letter, not the least stroke of a pen, will by any means disappear from the Law until everything is accomplished" (Matthew 5:18). Paul added, "All Scripture is God-breathed" (2 Timothy 3:16). Although human authors recorded the messages, "prophecy never had its origin in the will of man, but men spoke from God as they were carried along by the Holy Spirit" (2 Peter 1:20-21).

If God cannot be wrong and if the Bible is the Word of God, then the Bible cannot be wrong. God has spoken, and he has not stuttered. The God of truth has given us the Word of truth, and it does not contain any untruth. This is not to say that there are not *difficulties* in the Bible. But God's people can approach difficult texts with confidence, knowing that they are not actual errors.

Spiritual But Not Literal?

Some have suggested that Scripture can be trusted on matters of faith and life, but it is not always correct on historical matters. If true, this would make the Bible ineffective as a divine authority, for the historical and scientific is inextricably interwoven with the spiritual.

A close examination of Scripture reveals that the factual and spiritual truths of Scripture are often inseparable. We cannot separate the spiritual truth of Christ's resurrection from the fact that his body permanently and physically vacated the tomb and walked among people (Matthew 28:6; 1 Corinthians 15:13-19). If Jesus was not born of a biological virgin, then he is no different from the rest of the human race. Likewise, the death of Christ for our sins cannot be detached from the literal shedding of his blood on the cross (Hebrews 9:22). Adam's existence and fall cannot be a myth. If there were no literal Adam and no actual fall, then the spiritual teaching about inherited sin and physical and spiritual death are wrong (Romans 5:12). Historical reality and the theological doctrine stand or fall together.

Jesus often directly compared Old Testament events with important spiritual truths. Note the connections between the historical and spiritual lessons in the following passages:

- Matthew 12:40: "As Jonah was three days and three nights in the belly of a huge fish, so the Son of Man will be three days and three nights in the heart of the earth."

- Matthew 24:37-39: "As it was in the days of Noah, so it will be at the coming of the Son of Man. For in the days before the flood, people were eating and drinking, marrying and giving in marriage, up to the day Noah entered the ark; and they knew nothing about what would happen until the flood came and took them all away. That is how it will be at the coming of the Son of Man."

- John 3:12: "I have spoken to you of earthly things and you do not believe; how then will you believe if I speak of heavenly things?"

If the Bible does not speak truthfully about the physical world, it cannot be trusted when it speaks about the spiritual world. The two are intimately related.

Inspiration includes not only all that the Bible explicitly *teaches,* but everything the Bible *touches.* The Bible is God's Word, and God does not deviate from the truth. All the parts are as true as the whole they comprise.

What About Supposed Conflicts in the Bible?

Allegations of errors in the Bible are based on errors of their own. No informed person would claim to be able to fully explain all the difficult passages in the Bible. However, it is a mistake for the skeptic to assume that the unexplained cannot and will not be explained. When a scientist comes upon an anomaly in nature, he does not give up further scientific exploration. Rather, the unexplained motivates further study. Scientists once could not explain meteors, eclipses, tornadoes, hurricanes, and earthquakes, yet the unexplained motivated further research into the unknown.

The Bible should be researched with the same presumption that there are answers to the unexplained. Critics once proposed that Moses could not have written the first five books of the Bible because Moses' culture was preliterate. Now we know that writing had existed thousands of years before Moses.

Critics also once believed that Bible references to the Hittite people were fictional because archaeological evidence for the existence of the Hittites had never been found. When the Hittites' national library was unearthed in Turkey, that accusation fell flat. Liberal scholars once argued that certain Old Testament books could not have been written before the first century B.C. The discovery of the Dead Sea Scrolls proved that the prophecies from the Old Testament had existed long earlier than had been claimed. These and many more examples inspire confidence that the Bible difficulties that still remain are not mistakes or errors.

Some critics assume the Bible is guilty until proven innocent. However, as with an American citizen who is charged with a crime, the Bible should be read with at least the same presumption of accuracy given to other literature that claims to be nonfiction. This is the way we approach all human communications, and to treat the Bible otherwise would not be fair. And if we did not grant such presumption to the world around us, life would not be possible. For example, if we assumed that road signs and traffic signals were not telling the truth, it would lead to chaos. If we assumed food packages were mislabeled, we would have to open all cans and packages of food before buying them.

The Bible, like any other book, should be presumed to be telling us what the authors said, experienced, and heard. Negative critics begin with just the opposite presumption. It's little wonder they conclude the Bible is riddled with errors.

As an infallible book, the Bible is also irrevocable. Jesus declared, "Truly I say to you, until heaven and earth pass away, not the smallest letter or stroke shall pass away from the Law until all is accomplished" (Matthew 5:18 NASB). The Scriptures also have final authority, serving as the last word on all it discusses. Jesus employed the Bible to resist the tempter (Matthew 4:4,7,10), to settle doctrinal disputes (Matthew 21:42), and to vindicate his authority (Mark 11:17). Sometimes a biblical teaching rests on a small historical detail (Hebrews 7:4-10), a word or phrase (Acts 15:13-17), or the difference between the singular and the plural (Galatians 3:16).

While the Bible is infallible, human interpretations are not. Even though God's Word is perfect (Psalm 19:7), as long as imperfect human beings exist, there will be misinterpretations of God's Word.

Navigating Alleged Bible Contradictions

Critics of the Bible jump to the conclusion that a *partial* report is a *wrong* report. However, this is not the case. If it were, most of what has ever been said would be false, since seldom does time or space permit an absolutely complete report about something. Occasionally Bible writers expressed the same thing in different ways, stressing different things. For example, the four Gospels relate the same basic story—and often the same incidents—in different ways to different groups of people. And sometimes the same saying is quoted in two different places, using different words.

For example, let's look at Peter's confession of Christ in the following three Gospels:

- Matthew 16:16: "You are the Christ, the Son of the living God."

- Mark 8:29: "'But what about you?' he asked. 'Who do you say I am?' Peter answered, 'You are the Christ.'"

- Luke 9:20: "'But what about you?' he asked. 'Who do you say I am?' Peter answered, 'The Christ of God.'"

In each case there is a slight variation in Peter's words, but the intended meaning is the same. Rather than a deliberate attempt to deceive, the writers simply retell the story using slightly different words.

If such important topics can be stated in different ways, then there is no reason the same cannot be true for all the rest of Scripture.

Others point to variations in the New Testament citations of Old Testament scriptures as a proof of errors. They forget that every *citation* need not be an exact *quotation*. Sometimes people today use both indirect and direct quotations. It is perfectly acceptable to give the *essence* of a statement without using precisely the *same words*. The same *meaning* can be conveyed without using the same exact *verbal expressions*. Yet in no case does the New Testament misinterpret or misapply the Old Testament, nor draw an invalid implication from it. The New Testament makes no mistakes when it cites the Old Testament.

Some claim that because two or more accounts of the same event differ, that at least one of the accounts is inaccurate. For example, Matthew 28:5 says there was one angel at Jesus' tomb after the resurrection, while John informs us there were two (20:12). But these are not contradictory reports. The fact that Matthew mentions only one angel does not mean there could not be another.

Another classic variance is found when we compare Matthew 27:5 to Acts 1:18.

- Matthew 27:5: "Judas threw the money into the temple and left. Then he went away and hanged himself."

- Acts 1:18: "With the reward he got for his wickedness, Judas bought a field; there he fell headlong, his body burst open and all his intestines spilled out."

Matthew informs us that Judas hanged himself. But Luke says that he fell, his body burst open, and all his entrails gushed out (Acts 1:18). Once more, these accounts are not mutually exclusive. If Judas hanged himself from a tree over the edge of a cliff or gully in a rocky area, and his body fell on sharp rocks below, then it would make sense that his entrails would gush out, just as Luke described.

The Bible was written for the common person rather than as a scientific manual. Because of this, some claim that the Bible contains errors because it speaks of the sun rising, for instance, even though the sun does not move, but rather the earth. However, the Scriptures were written in *ancient* times by ancient standards, and it would be unfair to impose scientific standards upon it. Besides, it is *very* common for people even today to speak of the sun*rise* and sun*set,* though it's the earth that moves and not the sun.

But Can Every Detail Be True?

Some argue that Scripture is inaccurate in its use of numbers. For instance, the Bible often uses round numbers (Joshua 3:4; 4:13). It refers to the diameter of something as being about one-third of the circumference of something (1 Chronicles 19:18; 21:5). Just because an *approximation* is given does not mean it is *incorrect.* An approximation is sufficient for a "cast metal" sea (2 Chronicles 4:2) in an ancient Hebrew temple, though it would not suffice for a computer in a rocket. However, we should not expect to see people in a prescientific era always use precise numbers when recounting an event.

In regard to accuracy, critics have also failed to consider that one work can include different types of speech within it. For example, the books of Job, Psalms, and Proverbs are poetry. And the Synoptic Gospels feature *parables.*

It is not a mistake for a biblical writer to use a figure of speech, but rather it is a mistake for a reader to insist on taking a figure of speech literally. Obviously when the Bible speaks of a person resting under the shadow of God's wings (Psalm 36:7) it is not saying that God is a feathered bird.

Some argue that the text of the Bible is flawed because some of the early manuscripts contain mistakes. Yet God only inspired the *original* text of Scripture, not the copies. Therefore, only the original text is without error. Inspiration does not guarantee that every copy is without error, especially copies made from copies made from copies made from copies. Therefore, we are to expect that minor errors can occur in manuscripts.

For example, 2 Kings 8:26 says Ahaziah became king at age 22, while some versions of 2 Chronicles 22:2 say he was 42 when he ascended the throne. The latter number cannot be correct, or he would have been older than his father. This is obviously a copyist error, and it does not mean the original text was flawed.

We should not assume that errors found in the copies are errors that came from the originals. Also, none of the *minor* errors that have been found in copies change any of the major teachings. The copyist errors that have been found are relatively few in number. And usually, by looking at the context, we can determine which one is inaccurate. Finally, even when a copyist error occurs, the intended message always comes through.

Critics often jump to the conclusion that unqualified statements leave no room for exceptions. The book of Proverbs has many of these. Proverbial sayings, by their very nature, offer general guidance, not universal assurance. They are basic rules for life, and because they are basic, they allow room for exceptions. For example, Proverbs 16:7 affirms that "when a man's ways are pleasing to the LORD, he makes even his enemies live at peace with him." This obviously was not intended to be taken as a universal truth. Paul was pleasing to the Lord, and his enemies stoned him (Acts 14:19). Jesus was pleasing to the Lord, and his enemies crucified him. Nonetheless, it is a *general* truth that one who acts in a way that pleases God can minimize his enemies' antagonism. Wisdom literature applies God's universal truths to life's changing circumstances. The results will not always be the same, but the principles are helpful guides.

Then there is what theologians call *progressive revelation*. God does not reveal everything at once, nor does he lay down the same conditions for every period of history. Some of his later revelations will supersede his earlier statements. Bible critics sometimes confuse a *change* in revelation with a *mistake*. That a parent allows a very small child to eat with his fingers but demands that an older child use a fork is not a contradiction. This is considered a progression, with each command suited to the circumstance.

There was a time when God tested the human race by forbidding people to eat of a specific tree in the Garden of Eden (Genesis 2:16-17). This command is no longer in force, but the later revelation does not contradict this former revelation. Also, there was a period (under the Mosaic law) when God commanded that animals be sacrificed for people's sins. However, because Christ has offered the perfect sacrifice for sin (Hebrews 10:11-14), this Old Testament command is no longer in effect. Even then, there is no contradiction between the former and later commands.

Now What?

In Galatians 1:8 the apostle Paul instructed, "Even if we or an angel from heaven should preach a gospel other than the one we preached to you, let him be eternally condemned!" According to this verse, we should not allow anyone to deceive us into believing the gospel is anything less or different than the revealed Word of God.

The next part of our investigation will take a closer look at the accuracy of the Bible. Though many people consider the Bible sacred, few know the facts about how well its words have been preserved over the centuries and why such preservation is important. If we believe God's Word is true, then it is vital to understand how it has been transmitted from the original writings to the copies we use today.

PART TWO:

How Accurate Is the Bible?

THE HISTORICAL CREDIBILITY OF THE BIBLE:
What Evidence Exists for Its Claims?

C hristians and skeptical non-Christians have different views concerning the historical credibility of the Bible. For the Christian at least, nothing is more vital than the words of Jesus himself, who promised, "Heaven and earth will pass away, but my words will never pass away" (Matthew 24:35). If Christ's words were not accurately recorded in the Gospels, for instance, how can anyone know what he really taught? The truth is, we couldn't know. Further, if the remainder of the New Testament cannot be established to be historically reliable, then little if anything can be known about what true Christianity really is, teaches, or means.

Whereas Christians accept the claims the Bible makes for itself, skeptics usually approach the Bible from a rationalistic viewpoint, discounting its supernatural elements and often claiming that the New Testament books were not even written until the late first or early second century.

In this chapter, we'll begin by surveying the critical view, particularly of the New Testament, by those involved in academic circles, such as the members of the Jesus Seminar. We will then counter the critical view with an investigation based on historical research available from today's leading authorities on the Bible.

Understanding the Critical View

The skeptics' argument, usually based on the use of higher critical methods, is often given as follows: By a number of criteria the reliability of the New Testament text may be reasonably doubted. This includes the so-called mythological character of the Bible, the alleged findings of what is labeled "the criteria of dissimilarity" and of higher criticism in general, such as the probability of textual corruption through either the early church (oral tradition, source, or form criticism) or a later editor.

Additional allegations include the fabrication of a fictitious view of Jesus on the basis of a coming Jewish Messiah; the hundreds of thousands of variants in extant texts; the dubious theological embellishments of the apostle Paul (such as in his view of salvation through Jesus Christ); and the invention of most of the teachings of Christ to suit the spiritual or other needs of the early church, or even the removal of the actual teachings of Christ in later church councils for the purpose of politics or theological bias. The Jesus Seminar, for example, widely employs the "dissimilarity principle" to supposedly determine what Jesus actually said. According to the Jesus Seminar, a text or saying is reliable only when it *contrasts* with the thinking of the early Christians. They reason that odd or unusual sayings are unlikely to have been invented by the Gospel writers, and thus are probably authentic.

Thomas C. Oden provides a common view of Jesus held by many modern scholars:

> Jesus was an eschatological prophet [meaning he spoke about events that will take place at the end of history] who proclaimed God's coming kingdom and called his hearers to decide now for or against the kingdom. After he was condemned to death and died, the belief emerged gradually that he had risen. Only after some extended period of time did the remembering community develop the idea that Jesus would return as the Messiah, Son of Man. Eventually

this community came to project its eschatological expectation back upon the historical Jesus, inserting in his mouth the eschatological hopes that it had subsequently developed but now deftly had to rearrange so as to make it seem as if Jesus Himself had understood himself as Messiah. Only much later did the Hellenistic idea of the God-man, the virgin birth, and incarnation emerge in the minds of the remembering church, who again misremembered Jesus according to its revised eschatological expectation.[1]

James W. Sire, who cites this view, remarks,

> Oden in the following eight pages shows how and why this "modern view" is seriously at odds with reason.…. How such a vacuous implausible interpretation could have come to be widely accepted is itself perplexing enough. Even harder to understand is the thought that the earliest rememberers would actually suffer martyrdom for such a flimsy cause. One wonders how those deluded believers of early centuries gained the courage to risk passage into an unknown world to proclaim this message that came from an imagined revolution of a fantasized Mediator. The "critical" premise itself requires a high degree of gullibility.[2]

The conservative view of Scripture takes quite another approach. It maintains that, on the basis of accepted internal and external evidence, the biblical text can be established to be reliable history in spite of the novel and biased speculations of critics. Textually, there is simply no legitimate basis upon which to doubt the credibility and accuracy of the New Testament writers. Further, the methods used by the critics (higher critical methods) have been weighed in the balance even of secular scholarship and been found wanting. Their method of biblical analysis is factually false. Even in a positive sense the fruit they have borne is minuscule while, negatively, they are responsible for a tremendous amount of destruction relative to people's confusion over biblical authority and their confidence in the Bible.

In this sense, the critics conform to the warnings of Chauncey Sanders, associate professor of military history at The Air University, Maxwell Air Force Base, Montgomery, Alabama. In his book *An Introduction to Research in English Literary History,* Sanders warns the literary critic to be certain that he or she is also careful to examine the evidence *against* his case:

> He must be as careful to collect evidence against his theory as for it. It may go against the grain to be very assiduous in searching for ammunition to destroy one's own case; but it must be remembered that the overlooking of a single detail may be fatal to one's whole argument. Moreover, it is the business of the scholar to seek the truth, and the satisfaction of having found it should be ample recompense for having to give up a cherished but untenable theory.[3]

Ten Key Facts Regarding the New Testament's Historical Reliability

In our research, which includes decades of discussion with some of the world's top biblical scholars, we have discovered there are ten key facts that lend support to the reliability of the material we find in our New Testament.

Fact One: The Bibliographical Test

The historical accuracy of the New Testament can be proven by subjecting it to three generally accepted tests for determining historical reliability. Such tests are utilized in literary criticism and the study of historical documents in general. They involve (1) bibliographical, (2) internal, and (3) external examinations of the text and other evidence.

The bibliographical test seeks to determine whether we can reconstruct the original manuscript from the earliest copies at hand. For the New Testament we have 5700 Greek manuscripts and manuscript portions, 10,000 Latin Vulgate, 9300 other versions, plus

36,000 early (A.D. 100–300) quotations of the New Testament from the early church fathers—such that all but a few verses of the entire New Testament could be reconstructed from these alone.[4] What does this mean? Few scholars question the general reliability even of ancient classical literature written by Aristotle or Plato on the basis of the manuscripts we possess. Yet the number of manuscripts that have survived ancient classical writers are vastly inferior to that of the New Testament manuscripts. For example, of 16 well-known classical authors, such as Plutarch, Tacitus, Suetonius, Polybius, Thucydides, and Xenophon, the total number of extant copies is typically *less* than ten and the earliest copies date from 750 to 1600 years *after* the original manuscript was first penned.[5] We need only compare such slim evidence to the mass of biblical documentation, which includes over 24,000 manuscript portions, manuscripts, and versions, with the earliest fragments and complete copies surviving from between 50 and 300 years after they were originally written by the apostles and their associates.

Given the fact that the early Greek manuscripts date much closer to the originals than for any other ancient literature and given the overwhelming additional abundance of manuscripts available, any doubt as to the integrity or authenticity of the New Testament text has been removed—no matter what so-called "higher" critics claim. Indeed, this kind of evidence supplied by the New Testament (both quantity and quality) is the dream of the historian. No other ancient literature has ever come close to supplying such an abundance of data.

It is this wealth of material that has enabled scholars to place the restoration of the original New Testament text at 99 percent plus.[6] That is, they are sure we now have 99 percent of what the New Testament writers wrote. The one percent in doubt has no bearing on essential Christian teachings. No other document of the ancient period has been as accurately preserved as the New Testament.

Scholars are satisfied that they possess substantially the true text of the principal Greek and Roman writers whose works have come down to us—writers such as Sophocles, Thucydides, Cicero, and Virgil. Yet their satisfaction rests on a mere handful of manuscripts, whereas the manuscripts of the New Testament are counted by hundreds and even thousands.[7]

In other words, those who question the reliability of the New Testament must also question the reliability of virtually every ancient writing in the world because no other text has a similar abundance of evidence to support it. How can one logically reject the New Testament when its documentation is hundreds of times better than that of other ancient literature?

Fact Two: The Internal Evidence Test

This test asserts that we can assume the truthful reporting of an ancient document unless the facts indicate otherwise. Some call this the "innocent until proven guilty" test. For example, do the New Testament writers contradict themselves? Is there anything in their writings that causes us to objectively suspect their trustworthiness?

The answer is no. There is no proof of fraud or error on the part of *any* New Testament writer. But there *is* evidence of careful eyewitness reporting throughout the New Testament. The caution exercised by the writers, their personal convictions and claims that what they wrote was true, and the lack of demonstrable errors or contradictions indicate that the Gospel authors and, indeed, all the New Testament authors pass the second test as well (Luke 1:1-4; John 19:35; 21:24; Acts 1:1-3; 2:22; 26:24-26; 2 Peter 1:16; 1 John 1:1-3).

Further, the kinds of details the Gospel writers included in their narratives offer strong evidence for their integrity. They recorded their own faults and failures, even serious sins (Matthew 26:56,69-75; Mark 10:35-45). They did not hesitate to record even the most difficult and consequential statements of Jesus, such as John 6:41-71. They forthrightly supplied the embarrassing and even capital charges of Jesus' own enemies. Even though Jesus was their Messiah and Lord, they not only recorded the charges that Jesus broke the Sabbath but also that he was called a blasphemer and a liar, insane, and demon-possessed (Matthew 26:65; John 7:20,47; 8:48,52; 10:20).

To encounter such honesty from those who loved the person they were reporting about gives us an extremely high level of confidence that the Gospel writers placed a high premium on truthfulness.

Fact Three: The External Evidence Test

This test seeks either to corroborate or to falsify the documents on the basis of additional historical literature and data. (In this section we will look at Christian sources, and in fact four we will look at non-Christian sources.) Is there corroborating evidence for the claims made in the New Testament found *outside* the New Testament? Or are the claims or events of the New Testament successfully refuted by other competent first-century eyewitness reports? Are there statements in the New Testament that can be proved false according to known archaeological, historical, or literary evidence from that same time period?

The New Testament again passes the test. For example, Luke wrote approximately one-fourth of the New Testament. His careful historical writing has been affirmed through detailed personal archaeological investigation by former critic Sir William Ramsay, who stated after his painstaking research, "Luke's history is unsurpassed in respect of its trustworthiness."[8] A.N. Sherwin-White, the distinguished historian of Rome, stated of Luke, "For [the book of] Acts the confirmation of historicity is overwhelming. Any attempt to reject its basic historicity even in matters of detail must now appear absurd."[9]

Papias, a student of the apostle John and Bishop of Hierapolis around A.D. 150, observed that the apostle John himself noted that Mark, in writing his Gospel, "wrote down *accurately*...whatsoever he [Peter] remembered of the things said or done by Christ. Mark committed *no* error...for he was *careful of one thing,* not to omit any of the things he [Peter] had heard, and not to state any of them *falsely."*[10] Further, fragments of Papias's *Exposition of the Oracles of the Lord* (A.D. 140, III, XIX, XX) assert that the Gospels of Matthew, Mark, and John are all based on reliable eyewitness testimony (his portion on Luke is missing).[11]

Even centuries of scholarly biblical criticism have not proven that the writers of the Bible were anything other than careful and honest reporters of the events recorded.

Fact Four: The Evidence from Non-Christian Sources

The existence of both Jewish and secular accounts help confirm the picture of Christ that is presented in the New Testament. Scholarly research, such as that by Dr. Gary R. Habermas in *Ancient Evidence for the Life of Jesus,* indicates that "a broad outline of the life of Jesus" and his death by crucifixion can be reasonably and directly inferred from entirely non-Christian sources.[12] He cites 17 ancient non-Christian writings that provide specific information about Jesus and Christianity.

Using only the information gleaned from these ancient extrabiblical sources, what can we conclude concerning the death and resurrection of Jesus? Can these events be historically established based on these sources alone? Of the 17 documents examined by Dr. Habermas, 11 different works speak of the death of Jesus in

Habermas's 17 Ancient Sources:
1. Tacitus (55–120)
2. Suetonius (117–138)
3. Josephus (37–97)
4. Thallus (wrote c. 52)
5. Pliny the Younger (wrote c. 112)
6. Emperor Trajan (wrote c. 112)
7. Emperor Hadrian (wrote c. 117–138)
8. The Talmud (organized by 135)
9. Toledoth Jesu (exact date unknown)
10. Lucian (second century)
11. Mara Bar-Serapion (likely second century)
12. The Gospel of Truth (135–160)
13. The Apocryphon of John (120–130)
14. The Gospel of Thomas (140–200)
15. The Treatise on Resurrection (mid to late second century)
16. Acts of Pontius Pilate (lost work cited by Justin Martyr in 150)
17. Phlegon (noted by Origen as writing about Jesus in the early second century)

varying amounts of detail, with five of these specifying crucifixion as the method. When these sources are examined using the normal historical procedures used with other ancient documents, the result is conclusive.[13]

Fact Five: The Evidence of Archaeology

Detailed archaeological confirmation exists for the Bible and especially for the New Testament documents. Dr. Clifford Wilson is the former director of the Australian Institute of Archaeology and author of *New Light on the New Testament Letters; New Light on the Gospels; Rock, Relics* and *Biblical Reliability.* In his 17-volume set on the archaeological confirmation of the Bible he writes, "Those who know the facts now recognize that the New Testament must be accepted as a remarkably accurate source book."[14] We will discuss this further in a later chapter.

Fact Six: The Silence of Christianity's Critics

The complete inability of the many enemies of Jesus and the early church to discredit early Christian claims when they had both the motive and ability to do so argues strongly for the truthfulness of those claims. This silence does not prove Christianity itself is true, but it does prove that early evidence for discrediting the Christian movement was lacking.

Fact Seven: Numerous Eyewitness Accounts

The presence of numerous eyewitnesses to the events recorded in the New Testament would surely have prohibited any alteration or distortion of the facts, just as today false reporting as to the events of the Vietnam War or War on Terror would be corrected on the basis of living eyewitnesses and historical records.

Some argue that the Gospel writers' reporting of miracles cannot be trusted because they were only giving their subjective experience of Jesus rather than objectively reporting real miraculous events. They *thought* Jesus did miracles, but were mistaken. What is ignored by critics is what the texts plainly state. These miracles were done openly before both friends and enemies, not in a corner (Acts 26:26). Multitudes were literally eyewitnesses of the miraculous nature and deeds of Jesus (Luke 1:2; Acts 2:32; 4:20; 2 Peter 1:16), and their testimony should be believed *because* it was true (John 20:30-31; 21:24). Remember how Peter addressed over 3000 Jews in Jerusalem only five weeks after Jesus had been crucified? Then Peter stood up with the other disciples and addressed the crowd: "Fellow Jews and all of you who live in Jerusalem, let me explain this to you; listen carefully to what I say…Men of Israel, listen to this: Jesus of Nazareth was a man accredited by God to you by miracles, wonders and signs, which God did among you through him, as you yourselves know" (Acts 2:14,22).

In fact, the New Testament authors wrote that Jesus himself presented his miracles in support of his claims to be both the prophesied Messiah and God in human form. In Mark 2:8-11, when Jesus healed the paralyzed man, he did it so "that you may know that the Son of Man has authority on earth to forgive sins"—a clear claim to being God. In John 10:33, when the Jews accused Jesus of blasphemy because as supposedly only a man he was yet claiming to be God, what was Jesus' response? "Do not believe me unless I do what my Father does. But if I do it, even though you do not believe me, believe the miracles, that you may know and understand that the Father is in me, and I in the Father" (John 10:37-38). When John the Baptist was in jail and apparently had doubts as to whether Jesus was the Messiah, what did Jesus do? He told John's disciples to go and report about the miracles he did, which were in fulfillment of specific messianic prophecy (Matthew 11:2-5) in the Old Testament, cited by the Essenes at Qumran.[15]

The truth is that the teachings and miracles of Jesus are so intricately bound together that if we remove the miracles, we must discard Jesus' teachings.

Fact Eight: Corroboration from Date of Authorship

The fact that both conservative and liberal religious scholars have authored defenses of an early date for the writing of the New Testament is a witness to the strength of the evidence for an early date. For example, in *Redating Matthew, Mark & Luke,* noted conservative British scholar John Wenham presents a strong case that the first three Gospels were written before A.D. 55. He dates Matthew at A.D. 40 (some tradition says the early 30s), Mark at A.D. 45, and Luke no later than A.D. 51–55.[16]

Even liberal bishop John A.T. Robinson argued in his *Redating the New Testament* that the entire New Testament was written and in circulation between A.D. 40 and 65.[17] To some critical scholars, it is becoming an increasingly persuasive argument that all the New Testament books were written before A.D. 70—within a single generation of the death of Christ.

The implications of this fact are substantial. A New Testament written entirely in the first century virtually destroys the idea that later legends about Jesus became the basis of Christianity and the New Testament. What the New Testament reports, it reports accurately.

Further, it means the information must be accurate and truthful because it was written when both friend and enemies (who had witnessed Jesus' life and actions) were still alive. If the information was wrong, both sides would have gladly pointed that out. Why? Because those who knew and loved Jesus would not put up with any false information. And those who hated Jesus would have been glad to discredit him if they could. As it was, neither side could disagree with the information.

Fact Nine: Corroboration from Critical Methods Themselves

Even the methods of criticism indirectly support New Testament reliability. Although higher-critical theories in general reject biblical reliability based on a predetermined bias, when such theories "are subjected to the same analytical scrutiny as they apply to the New Testament documents they will be found to make their own contribution to validating the historicity of those records."[18]

Fact Ten: Confirmation from Legal Testimony and Skeptics

Finally, we find evidence in the historicity of the Bible when we consider the fact that many great minds of legal history have, on the grounds of strict legal evidence alone, accepted the New Testament as reliable history—not to mention the fact that many brilliant, skeptical intellects in the past and today have converted to Christianity on the basis of the historical evidence (including Saul of Tarsus, Athenagoras, Augustine, George Lyttleton, Gilbert West, C.S. Lewis, Frank Morison, Sir William Ramsay, and John Warwick Montgomery).

Lawyers are expertly trained in the matter of evaluating evidence and are perhaps the most qualified in the task of weighing data critically. The greatest authority in English and American common-law evidence in the nineteenth century, Harvard Law School professor Simon Greenleaf, wrote *Testimony of the Evangelists,* in which he powerfully demonstrated the reliability of the Gospels.[19] In addition, Irwin Linton, who represented cases before the Supreme Court and wrote *A Lawyer Examines the Bible,* stated:

> So invariable had been my observation that he who does not accept wholeheartedly the evangelical, conservative belief in Christ and the Scriptures has never read, has forgotten, or never been able to weigh—and certainly is utterly unable to refute—the irresistible force of the cumulative evidence upon which such faith rests, that there seems ample ground for the conclusion that such ignorance is an invariable element in such unbelief. And this is so even though the unbeliever be a preacher, who is supposed to know this subject if he know no other.[20]

What of hundreds of contemporary lawyers who, on the grounds of strict legal evidence, accept the New Testament as historically reliable? We must emphasize that to reject the New Testament accounts as true history is, by definition, to reject the canons of legitimate historical study. If this cannot be done, the New Testament must be retained as careful historical reporting.

The New Testament has proven itself reliable in the crucible of history. It is rather skeptics who have been unable to prove their case. Nor are the implications small. Legal scholar J.N.D. Anderson observes in *Christianity: The Witness of History:*

> ...it seems to me inescapable that anyone who chanced to read the pages of the New Testament for the first time would come away with one overwhelming impression—that here is a faith firmly rooted in certain allegedly historical events, a faith which would be false and misleading if those events had not actually taken place, but which, if they did take place, is unique in its relevance and exclusive in its demands on our allegiance. For these events did not merely set a "process in motion and then themselves sink back into the past. The unique historical origin of Christianity is ascribed permanent, authoritative, absolute significance; what happened once is said to have happened once for all and therefore to have continuous efficacy."[21]

The Bible is not ancient fiction, but rather the historical reporting of the most significant events in human history—including the life, death, and resurrection of Jesus Christ, the founder of the Christian faith and God in human form.

5

THE INERRANCY OF THE BIBLE:
How Can We Say God's Word Is Perfect?

What is your opinion on the authority of the Bible? Do you see it as the literal Word of God? Many have viewed it as only the humanly inspired words of great writers from which we are free to pick and choose what we will accept or reject. Others suggest the Bible is a combination of divine words and human beliefs.

In this chapter, we will tackle the important subject of biblical inerrancy—the claim that the Bible is without error and is 100 percent perfect in its original texts. We begin by first asking…

Why Is Biblical Inerrancy Such an Important Issue?

Simply put, the matter of inerrancy is important because of its implications. The Bible claims to be perfect, and Jesus Christ claimed the Bible was without error. If the Bible claims it is inerrant and is wrong, then the Bible contains error on a critical subject: its own authority.

But then Jesus would also be wrong. If the Bible and Jesus were both wrong on this point, they could have been wrong on any point. Without inerrancy, subjectivism and uncertainty concerning divine revelation can result in either agnosticism or blind trust on any given passage or teaching of Scripture. In other words, if the Bible contains errors, how can we be certain we are able to determine where it speaks truth and where it speaks error?

On the other hand, if a reasonable defense of inerrancy can be made, then, given the conditions under which the Bible was written, it is extremely difficult to reject the idea that the Bible is the inspired Word of God. The Bible was written in Hebrew and Greek, two very different languages (plus some Aramaic), by over 40 different authors from many walks of life over a vast period of time. It was not written by a single author over a period of just a few years.

Instead, the Bible was painstakingly hand-copied on perishable materials. It was not typed with a modern computer on high-quality reading paper. Over a period of 3000 years—from 1500 B.C. to A.D. 1600, the parchment upon which the Bible was written was frequently subjected to the stresses of weather, human neglect, political and military upheavals, and deliberate sabotage. It was not protected in a modern climate-controlled library. Given these and other adverse conditions, if the Bible was written only via human strength, it would necessarily contain numerous errors. But if it is actually without error, then given the thousands of details in its contents, such accuracy cannot reasonably be accounted for apart from divine inspiration and preservation.

Why Should We Investigate the Authority of the Bible?

Investigation of the Bible's claims is vital because of its teachings. The Bible is the single most influential book in the world. Simply due to its worldwide influence, every person should have a basic understanding of its teachings.

If the Bible is the Word of God, then its value to every person and every culture is of utmost importance. If it authoritatively answers the fundamental questions of life, then who can ignore its message? Only the Bible authoritatively answers these fundamental questions:

- Why are we here?
- Where did we come from?
- What is the nature of God?
- What is the remedy for sin?
- What happens when we die?

Who would *not* be interested in the answers?

Whatever one's view of the Bible, it stands as written and can be carefully investigated and evaluated by anyone who wishes. We think it is significant, given 2000 years of the most intense scrutiny by critics and skeptics, that millions of people in today's world continue to believe the Bible is the literal, inerrant Word of God.

A generation ago, when someone said, "I believe in the inspiration of the Bible," the meaning was generally understood. It meant this person believed the Bible was without error. As this belief has become increasingly questioned, however, the list of descriptive adjectives required to say the same thing has grown much longer.

Now, some who claim to believe in the Bible have narrowed their meaning of the inerrancy of Scripture to *exclude*...

- that individual words were inspired
- that the entire Bible was inspired
- that Scripture is inspired in all its parts rather than only in matters of faith

This idea of limited inerrancy, however, fails to address key theological issues. As we will soon discuss, limited inerrancy collapses on two fronts. First, the Bible makes no such distinction; it rather assumes full inerrancy. Second, the theological parts of the Bible are inseparable from the nontheological portions. In other words, if we accept that there are errors of science and history, it is impossible to maintain inerrancy in matters of faith and practice.

This inseparability can be illustrated with an example from the area of history regarding Jesus' resurrection. For instance, the Bible communicates that the resurrection took place in space-time history, not in terms of a religious allegory or myth (1 Corinthians 15:4-8). The resurrection is proof of Christ's role as Messiah (Luke 24:44-47), as God in human form (Philippians 2:1-10), and of coming divine judgment (Acts 17:31). Clearly then, the historical aspect of the resurrection is inseparably related to matters of faith and practice. It is therefore logically impossible to maintain the limited inerrancy view—that the Bible is without error only in its doctrinal and moral teachings, but contains error in matters of history.

If the credibility of Christian teaching and morality is directly related to the credibility of what the Bible teaches historically, then how can the teachings based upon faulty history be considered credible? In other words, to charge one with error is to implicate the other with error. There is no escaping this conclusion.

In addition, note that the resurrection, besides being a historical event, is also a miraculous event. As such, it challenges the domain of science. Some believe science is the authority by which we judge alleged scientific error in the Bible, but because science is based on the knowable and repeatable in order to arrive at conclusions, it cannot deal with the category of miraculous events in history that are not repeatable.

However, in science today, with the discovery of big bang cosmology accompanied by the anthropic principle found in the universe, some scientists claim that a transcendent supernatural agent outside of space, time, energy, and mass brought the universe into existence at a single moment. This is something the Bible claims throughout: "We understand that the universe was formed at God's command, so that what is seen was not made out of what was visible" (Hebrews 11:3). Every major doctrine of Scripture is intimately tied to the supernatural. If miracles are considered a priori impossible, then it follows that Christianity is clearly false, for miracles are assumed impossible by definition. Therefore, no God exists, and Jesus was only a man.

But many intellectuals have written about the inadequacies of science to dictate what may or may not take place in the universe. The proper way of investigating claims of a miraculous nature is via historical research that is open to following the evidence wherever it may lead.

Does It Really Matter?

Many argue the entire issue is blown out of proportion. Is there really all that much difference between a person who believes the Bible is 100 percent perfect in all that it conveys and a person who sees it only as a guide for matters of faith? Both believe in the importance of the Bible. In the end, does it really matter?

We realize that people are at different levels of understanding concerning the Bible. What we desire to point out here is that the issue of the Bible's inerrancy is not a minor one. That's because the issue involves the character of God and the establishing of biblical authority. All Christians agree God is a God of truth and all-powerful. If God did inspire or permit errors in the original writings of the Bible, aren't there negative implications for his character and nature? Further, how can we know where the errors are? In the end, can God or any part of his word be trusted? And how can we be truly certain Scripture will provide all that Christians need for spiritual health if Christians themselves are not certain which parts they can believe or trust?

This issue is more crucial than it may seem at first glance. As esteemed Hebrew scholar Dr. Gleason Archer points out, the concepts of inerrancy and the redemption of those who follow Christ are more closely connected than some think:

> God's written revelation came in inerrant form, free from discrepancies or contradictions, and this inerrancy contributes to its achieving its saving purpose. If there were genuine mistakes of any sort in the original manuscripts, it would mean, obviously, that the Bible contains error along with truth. As such it would become subject to human

judgment, just like any other religious document. The validity of such judgment, of course, depends on the judge's own knowledge and wisdom. If he rejects the truth of the scriptural record simply because it seems to him to be unlikely or improbable, then he is in danger of eternal loss. The charge of scriptural self-contradiction or factual error is to be taken quite seriously; it cannot be brushed off as a matter of minor consequence. At stake is the credibility and reliability of the Bible as authentic revelation from God…. For this reason there is no such thing as an inconsequential scriptural error. If any part of the Bible can be proved to be in error, then any other part of it—including the doctrinal, theological parts—may also be in error.[1]

Further, inerrancy has implications for how we treat the Bible. Human words are perceived differently from words that come from God. We probably would not give up much when it comes to mere human words, but we may be willing to give our lives to follow those words we believe are of God.

The Historical Battle for the Bible's Inerrancy

The history of Christianity reveals that in every generation the church has dealt with one or more key theological issues integrally related to its own health and vitality. Various issues arose at different times as a result of attacks from critics, heretics, or enemies of Christianity, and the careful study of those issues led to greater understanding of biblical truth.

In the early era of the church (the first through fourth centuries A.D.), among the key issues that were debated were (1) how Jesus was both fully God and fully human, (2) the confirmation of the New Testament books, and (3) the Trinity. In the Middle Ages (fifth through fourteenth centuries) the key issue was atonement. In the Reformation era (sixteenth through seventeenth centuries) the concern was the nature of justification (by faith alone, not faith and works) and the preeminence of Scripture alone, not tradition and Scripture, as the final authority were reaffirmed. In the modern era (eighteenth through twentieth centuries) the question of biblical authority became the prominent issue. Today, in the postmodern era, the key issues under debate are whether absolute truth exists and whether there is only one way to God (through Jesus) or there are many ways.

Although challenges to biblical authority began to surface during the Renaissance period, such skepticism more fully emerged during the Enlightenment. As a result, for over a century, liberals and conservatives opposed one another over the issue of biblical inspiration and authority. However, not until the 1960s did the issue of inerrancy come to the forefront.

The debate over inerrancy represents a stand for the absolute authority and trustworthiness of Scripture. Again, perhaps no single issue is more important to the Christian church today. How the individual and the church view the Bible influences how the individual and the church view almost everything else. It influences one's perspective on the existence of truth, how to know God personally, and today's social and moral issues (war, poverty, sexual orientation, and the fragmentation of the traditional family unit).

The Specifics of Inerrancy

Though we have discussed inerrancy in general to this point, we have yet to take the time to define the specific details of what inerrancy claims and does not claim. While many struggle with accepting inerrancy as a concept, other Christians who believe in inerrancy often have questions regarding what this belief does and does not claim.

What Inerrancy Does Claim

1. Inerrancy claims an absolutely errorless original text. It means that what the Bible teaches is true, without a single error in the original manuscripts. Dr. Paul Feinberg defines inerrancy in this way:

Inerrancy means that when all facts are known, the Scriptures in their original autographs and properly interpreted
will be shown to be wholly true in everything that they
affirm, whether that has to do with doctrine or morality
or with the social, physical, or life sciences.[2]

A more concise definition would be, "What Scripture says, God
says—through human agents and without error."[3]

2. Inerrancy must also apply equally to all parts of Scripture as
it was originally written.

3. The proper way to interpret the Bible involves a respect for the
text as given until proven otherwise. In other words, due attention
is given to claims for biblical authority. Also, as much as possible,
interpretation must involve an objective and impartial methodology.
Inerrancy is related to the intent of Scripture. For example, when
the intent of the writer is to record a lie or error by someone (such
as with a false prophet or the devil), the fact of a lie or error can
hardly deny inerrancy. Inerrancy only affirms that what is recorded
is recorded accurately. What the Bible records must be distinguished
from what the Bible approves.

What Inerrancy Does Not Claim

1. Inerrancy does not claim to be absolutely proven. Inerrancy
cannot guarantee the final solution to every alleged problem passage.
Given the present limited state of human knowledge, no one can
logically expect proof when the means of proof are absent. Proof
of inerrancy is therefore limited by our present state of knowledge.
However, this does not deny or disprove inerrancy. The fact that so
many opportunities exist within the Bible to disprove inerrancy and
yet it remains capable of rational defense is remarkable.

2. Inerrancy does not refer to manuscript copies or translations.
Copies and translations may be considered inerrant only to the degree
they reproduce the originals. Nevertheless, an accurate translation,
based upon an over 99 percent original text, virtually reproduces the

originals, and the remaining one percent is present in the variant readings. We can confidently claim we have "inerrant originals and virtually inerrant copies." Or, as New Testament scholar Dr. Daniel Wallace has stated on our program, *The John Ankerberg Show,* we have the original text in the Bible or in the footnotes. Not a word of Scripture is missing or waiting to be discovered.

3. Inerrancy does not claim absolute precision. Approximations are not errors. For example, no one would argue it is an error to say the following:

- "I earned $40,000 last year" (it was really $40,200).
- "In 1998 I received my college degree" (it was May of 1998).
- "What a beautiful sunset" (the earth's rotation makes it appear as though the sun is setting).

Today, even on television or in newspapers, people often use approximations, or are technically imprecise when it comes to grammar, numbers, science, or history. This is also true of the biblical writers. Their purpose was to communicate, and they sometimes wrote in generalities rather than specifics. Inerrancy does not demand the Bible be written without generalities, or with technical precision.

For similar reasons, inerrancy does not require strict grammatical, semantic, numeric, or historic precision. Inerrancy does not exclude the use of nonliteral, figurative language (allegory, personification, hyperbole) or various literary genres (apocalyptic, drama, poetry, parable). To exclude such language or genres would rob Scripture of much of its richness and universal appeal. Also, inerrancy does not demand verbatim exactness when the New Testament quotes the Old. A New Testament author has the right to give the basic idea or summarize for purpose of brevity. Only if a New Testament quotation denied or contradicted an Old Testament scripture would there be an error, but this never occurs.

In a similar fashion, inerrancy does not demand that any given biblical event or account be exhaustively reported. As Dr. Charles Ryrie wrote, "The inerrancy of the Bible means simply that the Bible tells the truth. Truth can and does include approximations, free quotations, language of appearances, and different accounts of the same event as long as those do not contradict."[4]

We have discussed in this chapter the inerrancy of the Bible and the importance and relevance of this concept for our lives today. In our next chapter, we'll continue by evaluating an area of Scripture that again makes it unique from all other books in history—the prophecies of the Bible. We'll discover that the Bible includes many prophecies and that its record of the fulfillment of those prophecies only points to the supernatural power of an already amazingly accurate historical book.

6

THE PROPHECIES OF THE BIBLE:
How Accurate Are They?

Someone once said, "We should all be concerned about our future because we will have to spend the rest of our lives there."

In the movie version of *Jumper*, the lead actor accidentally discovers his ability to travel through space and time. While the film included some extremely realistic technical effects, those who watched knew that the actor's time travel was part of the acting and not part of reality.

However, one of the intriguing aspects of *Jumper* and other time-travel movies is the idea of knowing what will occur in the future. In the Bible, we find that God revealed the future to a number of prophets and apostles. Ezekiel, Daniel, the apostle John, and others were each shown events that would take place in the future or at the end of the world. Yet some critics say it's impossible for anyone to predict future events, just like it's impossible to travel through time.

Who would deny that the future affects us all? What man or woman alive would ever say his or her future is unimportant? This is why millions of people turn to the supernatural, whether astrologers, fortune tellers, or self-proclaimed religious prophets, because they long to know what their future holds.

Yet the ancient Hebrew prophets made startling predictions

about the future, predictions that should amaze anyone. Many of these predictions have already come true, providing convincing evidence that the Bible's remaining unfulfilled prophecies will eventually come true as well.

In this chapter, we'll note some of the major Bible prophecies that have been fulfilled. As we do, we'll find that the Bible has made predictions with 100 percent accuracy—an astounding feat unparalleled by any religious group outside Christianity.

Prophecy's Purpose—To Prove Who the True God Is

Many people today think that all religions are equally true and that it is somehow wrong to say there is only *one* true God. Jesus, however, declared there is only one true God and that he could be known personally: "This is eternal life: that they may know you, the only true God, and Jesus Christ whom you have sent" (John 17:3). How can a person know Jesus was right? One way is by the study of prophecy. A central purpose of biblical prophecy is to show men and women who the one true God is "so that all the peoples of the earth may know that the LORD is God and that there is no other" (1 Kings 8:60).

God challenges people to compare his predictions with all others. He teaches that his knowledge of the future is proof that he alone is the Lord. No one else has consistently told of things to come and also had them come true exactly as forecast. One writer notes:

> ...the fact of predictive prophecy brings, first of all, glory to God; for each prediction testifies to its Author's wisdom and sovereignty over the future. As Isaiah spoke forth to the Israelites of his day, "Who hath declared it from the beginning, that we may say, 'He is right?'"...Predictions point up His powers, as contrasted with those of any conceivable rivals...When Joshua spoke out in faith and foretold the miracle of the cutting off of the waters of the Jordan (Josh. 3:13), he assured his people, "Hereby ye shall know

that the living God is among you" (v. 10); and to this end the prediction itself contributed, just as did the subsequent miracle.[1]

God actually challenges us to test him so even skeptics will have no excuse for rejecting his predictions:

> I foretold the former things long ago, my mouth announced them and I made them known; then suddenly I acted, and they came to pass. For I knew how stubborn you were; the sinews of your neck were iron, your forehead was bronze. Therefore I told you these things long ago; before they happened I announced them to you so that you could not say, "My idols did them";…You have heard these things; look at them all. Will you not admit them? From now on I will tell you of new things, of hidden things unknown to you… You have not heard of them before today. So you cannot say, "Yes, I knew of them" (Isaiah 48:3-7).

Only the Bible provides completely accurate predictions about the future. This is one reason God emphatically warns people to not presumptuously speak of the future in his name. To do so brings dishonor to God when the prophecy fails and leads people to not trust in him. In the Old Testament the penalty for false prophecies was severe: "A prophet who presumes to speak in my name anything I have not commanded him to say, or a prophet who speaks in the name of other gods, must be put to death" (Deuteronomy 18:20).

The Importance of Prophecy

How can we know Bible prophecy is important?

First, prophecy makes up a substantial portion of the Bible. There are over 600 direct references in the Bible to prophecy and prophets. Approximately 27 percent of the entire Bible contains prophetic material, much of which has already come true. Only four of the 66 books of the Bible lack any prophecies (Ruth, the Song of

Solomon, Philemon, and 3 John). Even the short book of Jude mentions prophecy (Jude 14,17-18). "[o]ut of the OT's 23,210 verses, 6,641 contain predictive material, or 28 ½ percent. Out of the NT's 7,914 verses, 1,711 contain predictive material, or 21 ½ percent. So for the entire Bible's 31,124 verses, 8,352 contain predictive material, or 27 percent of the whole."[2]

Second, the fact God strongly urges the study of prophecy. The apostle Peter teaches we "will do well to pay attention to it" because the prophecies in the Bible are not merely human words, but the words of God:

> We have the word of the prophets made more certain, and you will do well to pay attention to it, as to a light shining in a dark place…Above all, you must understand that no prophecy of Scripture came about by the prophet's own interpretation. For prophecy never had its origin in the will of man, but men spoke from God as they were carried along by the Holy Spirit (2 Peter 1:19-21).

The apostle Paul wrote, "All Scripture is God-breathed and is useful for teaching, rebuking, correcting and training in righteousness, so that the man of God may be thoroughly equipped for every good work" (2 Timothy 3:16). If all Scripture is inspired by God and useful, then this must also apply to all prophecy, which is also Scripture.

Prophecy is also important because in Matthew 24, Jesus personally encouraged the study of it. When Jesus was speaking of future events, he was asked a question by his disciples: "Tell us," they said, "when will this happen, and what will be the sign of your coming and of the end of the age?" (Matthew 24:3). Jesus' answer clearly revealed his thoughts on prophecy. He answered their question directly and in detail, supplying a great deal of information about future events.

To get a sense of how much emphasis Jesus placed on prophecy, consider his words in Mark 13: "Watch out that no one deceives you…the end is still to come…You must be on your guard…So be on your guard; I have told you everything ahead of time…When you see these things happening, you know that it [my return] is near, right at the door…Be on guard! Be alert!…Therefore keep watch…What I say to you, I say to everyone: 'Watch!' " (Mark 13:5,7,9,23,29,33,35,37). In fact, Jesus never criticized his disciples for studying prophecy. Rather, he confronted them for ignoring it: "How foolish you are, and how slow of heart to believe all that the prophets have spoken!" (Luke 24:25).

In addition, Jesus taught that Old Testament predictions concerning himself were of special importance. He said, "This is what I told you while I was still with you: Everything must be fulfilled that is written about me in the Law of Moses, the Prophets and the Psalms" (Luke 24:44). Here and elsewhere, Jesus taught the entire Hebrew Bible was about him, predicting the events of his life in particular detail.

Probability and Fulfilled Prophecy

To illustrate the divine nature of Bible prophecy, let's look at specific prophecies related to Jesus and evaluate the probability of them coming true. Anyone can make predictions; that is easy. Having them fulfilled is another story entirely. The more statements you make about the future, and the greater the detail, the better the chances proportionately, even exponentially, that you will be proven wrong.

For example, imagine how difficult it would be for someone today to predict, 700 years in advance, the exact city in which a future U.S. president will be born. That means predicting the birthplace of someone who is president around A.D. 2700. That's what the prophet Micah did when he prophesied the birthplace of Jesus the Messiah 700 years before he was born (Micah 5:2).

How difficult do you think it would be to predict the kind of death a religious leader will experience 1000 years from today?

Could you predict today a specific method of execution not currently known—one that won't be invented for several hundred more years? That's what David did in 1000 B.C. when he wrote about crucifixion in Psalm 22.

How difficult would it be to predict, hundreds of years in advance, the specific date on which a great future leader will appear? That's what the prophet Daniel did 530 years before Christ appeared (Daniel 9:24-27).

How could someone arrange, in advance, to be born in a specific family (see Genesis 12:2-3 and Matthew 1)? How does someone pick, in advance, his parents and his birthplace?

It might be possible to fake one or two of these predictions, but it would be impossible for any person to arrange 25 such prophecies and fulfill *all* of them (and many others) in advance. If it can be proved that such prophecies were given hundreds of years in advance, and one person fulfilled *all* of them, then that person would logically be the predicted Messiah of the Old Testament. Only God can see into the future.

A Sampling of Jesus' Fulfillment of Messianic Prophecies

1. He will be born of a virgin (Isaiah 7:14; see Matthew 1:23)
2. He would live in Nazareth of Galilee (Isaiah 9:1-2; Matthew 2:23; 4:15)
3. He would occasion the massacre of Bethlehem's children (Jeremiah 31:15; see Matthew 2:18)
4. He would be anointed by the Holy Spirit (Isaiah 11:2; see Matthew 3:16-17)
5. He would be heralded by the Lord's special messenger, John the Baptist (Isaiah 40:3; Malachi 3:1; see Matthew 3:1-2)
6. His mission would include the Gentiles (Isaiah 42:1-3,6; see Matthew 12:18-21). But he would be rejected by the Jews, his own people (Psalm 118:22; see 1 Peter 2:7)
7. His ministry would include miracles (Isaiah 35:2-6; 61:1-2; see Matthew 9:35; Luke 4:16-21)
8. He would be the Shepherd struck with a sword, resulting in the sheep being scattered (Zechariah 13:7; see Matthew 26:31,56; Mark 14:27,49-50)

9. He would be betrayed by a friend for 30 pieces of silver (Zechariah 11:12-13; see Matthew 27:9-10)
10. He would die a humiliating death (Psalm 22; Isaiah 53)
11. He would know rejection (Isaiah 53:3; John 1:10-12; 7:5,48)
12. He would be silent before his accusers (Isaiah 53:7; Matthew 27:12-19)
13. He would be mocked (Psalm 22:7-8; Matthew 27:31)
14. He would have his hands and feet pierced (Psalm 22:16; Luke 23:33)
15. He would be crucified with thieves (Isaiah 53:12; Matthew 27:38)
16. He would pray for his persecutors (Isaiah 53:12; Luke 23:43)
17. His side would be pierced (Zechariah 12:10; John 19:34)
18. He would be buried in a rich man's tomb (Isaiah 53:9; Matthew 27:57-60)
19. He would have lots cast for his garments (Psalm 22:18; John 19:23-24)
20. He would be given vinegar and gall to drink (Psalm 69:21; see Matthew 27:34)
21. He would rise from the dead (Psalm 16:10; Mark 16:6; Acts 2:31)
22. He would be hated without a cause (Psalm 69:4; Isaiah 49:7; John 7:48; 15:25)
23. He would be rejected by the rulers (Psalm 118:22; Matthew 21:42; John 7:48)
24. He would ascend into heaven (Psalm 68:18; Acts 1:9)
25. He would sit down at God's right hand (Psalm 110:1; Hebrews 1:3), and in the future he will be presented with dominion over peoples of all nations and every language (Daniel 7:13-14; see Revelation 11:15).

Adapted from Norman Geisler and Ron Brooks, *When Skeptics Ask: A Handbook of Christian Evidences* (Wheaton, IL: Victor Books, 1990), pp. 114-15.

There are many more prophecies we could list. All those listed above refer only to Christ's first coming. God gave a great number of prophecies about the coming Messiah for at least two reasons: First, it would make identifying the Messiah easier. And second, it would make it impossible for an imposter to claim he was Jesus.

To illustrate, consider the following account adapted from a true story.

Soviet double agent "Condor" was a World War II traitor. He gave atomic secrets to the Russians and then fled to Mexico after the war. His conspirators arranged to help him by planning a meeting with the secretary of the Russian ambassador in Mexico City. Proper identification for both parties was vital.

"Condor" was to identify himself with six prearranged signs.

These instructions had been given to both the secretary and "Condor" so there would be no possibility of making a mistake. The signs were as follows: (1) Once in Mexico City the Russian spy was to write a note to the secretary, signing his name as I. Jackson; (2) after three days he was to go to the Plaza de Colon in Mexico City and (3) stand before the statue of Columbus, (4) with his middle finger placed in a guidebook. In addition, (5) when he was approached, he was to say it was a magnificent statue and that he was from Oklahoma. (6) The secretary was to then give him his passport.

The six prearranged signs worked. Why? With six identifying characteristics, it was impossible for the secretary not to identify "Condor" as the proper agent.

If that is true, think how impossible it would be not to identify the Messiah if we had been given not just six but dozens of major, specific prophecies and hundreds of minor, more general prophecies pointing to him.

Professor emeritus of science at Westmont College Peter Stoner has calculated the probability of one man fulfilling the major prophecies made concerning the Messiah. The estimates were worked out by 12 different classes of 600 college students.

The students carefully weighed all the factors, discussed each prophecy at length, and examined the various circumstances that might indicate that men had conspired together to fulfill a particular prophecy. They made their estimates conservative enough so that there was finally unanimous agreement even among the most skeptical students.

But then Professor Stoner took their estimates and made them even more conservative. He also encouraged other skeptics or scientists to make their own estimates to see if his conclusions were more than fair. Finally, he submitted his figures for review to a committee of the American Scientific Affiliation (ASA). Upon examination, they verified that his calculations were dependable and accurate in regard to the scientific material presented.[3]

For example, concerning Micah 5:2, where Micah prophesied

the Messiah would be born in Bethlehem, Stoner and his students determined the average population of Bethlehem from the time of Micah to the present. Then they divided that figure by the average population of the earth during the same period. They concluded that the chance of one man being born in Bethlehem was one in 2.8 x 105—or rounded, one in 300,000.

After examining only *eight* different prophecies, they conservatively estimated that the chance of one man fulfilling all eight prophecies was one in 10^{17}.

To explain how large the number 10^{17} is (a figure with 17 zeros), Stoner gave this illustration: Imagine covering the entire state of Texas with silver dollars to a level of two feet deep. The total number of silver dollars needed to cover the whole state is 10^{17}. Now, choose just one silver dollar, mark it, and drop it from an airplane flying over the state. Then thoroughly stir all the silver dollars all over the state.

When that has been done, blindfold one person, and tell him he can travel wherever he wishes in the state of Texas in an attempt to reach down into all those silver dollars and pull up the one that was marked. The chance of his finding that one silver dollar—in the entire state of Texas—would be the same as the chance the Old Testament prophets had for eight of their prophecies coming true about any one man in the future.

In practical terms, is there anyone who would fail to invest in a financial venture if the chance of failure were only one in 10^{17}? This is the kind of sure investment we are offered by God for belief in his Messiah.

Professor Stoner concluded, "The fulfillment of these eight prophecies alone proves that God inspired the writing of those prophecies to a definiteness which lacks only one chance in 10^{17} of being absolute."[4] Another way of saying this is that any person who minimizes or ignores the significance of these identifying signs being fulfilled by the Messiah is foolish.

But, of course, Jesus fulfilled many more than eight prophecies.

In another calculation, Stoner used 48 prophecies (even though he could have used as many as 456) and arrived at the extremely conservative estimate that the probability of 48 prophecies being fulfilled in one person is 10^{157}.[5]

How large is the number one in 10^{157}? Well, 10^{157} includes 157 zeros. Let's try to illustrate the size of this number, this time using electrons.

Electrons are very small objects. They are smaller than atoms. It would take 2.5 times 10^{15} of them, laid side by side, just to add up to one inch. If we counted four electrons every second and counted day and night, it would take us 19 million years just to count a line of electrons one inch long.

But how many electrons would we have to count if we were dealing with 10^{157} of them? Imagine building a solid ball of electrons that would extend in all directions from the earth a length of six billion light years. The distance in miles of just *one* light year is 6.4 trillion miles. That would be a big ball! But not big enough to measure 10^{157} electrons.

In order to do that, you must take that big ball of electrons measuring six billion light years long in all directions and multiply it by 6×10^{28}! How big is that? It's the length of the space required to store trillions and trillions and trillions of the same gigantic balls and more. In fact, the space required to store all of these balls combined together would just start to "scratch the surface" of the number of electrons we would need.

Assuming you have some idea of the number of electrons we are talking about, imagine marking just *one* of those electrons. Then stir them all up, and appoint a person to travel in a rocket for as long as he wants, anywhere he wants to go in that mass of electrons. Tell him to then find that one marked electron. What do you think his chances of success would be? One in 10^{157}.

Remember, this number represents the chance of only 48 prophecies coming true in one person. This affirms that it is absolutely impossible for anyone to have fulfilled all the Messianic prophecies solely by chance. In fact, a leading authority on probability theory, Emile Borel, states in his book *Probabilities and Life* that once we go past one chance in 10^{50} (from a human perspective), the probabilities are so small it's impossible to think they will ever occur.[6]

Here is yet another illustration. Imagine one ant traveling at the speed of only *one inch* every 15 billion years. If the ant could carry only one atom at a time, how many atoms could it move in 10^{157} years? It could, even at that incredibly slow speed, move all the atoms in 600,000 trillion, trillion, trillion, trillion universes the size of our universe a distance of 30 billion light years![7]

This means it is virtually impossible for the aforementioned 48 prophecies to be fulfilled by chance alone. And what happens when we consider the 456 prophecies concerning the life of Christ? The odds become even greater. This serves as substantial evidence that the prophecies in the Bible came from a supernatural source—the God of the Bible.

Prophecy reveals that the Bible is of divine origin. No other explanation accounts for the Bible's perfect track record when it comes to fulfilled prophecy.

7

THE CONTEXT OF THE BIBLE:
Did Other Historical Writers Agree with the New Testament?

We live in a world of instant information. As soon as a plane crashes, we hear or read about it on television or the Internet. Immediately after a key play ends a football game, we can watch an instant replay of what happened. With the right tools, we can pause live television, watch two or more channels at the same time, and even watch live television from our mobile phones.

Information didn't move as rapidly during biblical times. Without television, Internet, radio, and the mail systems of today, news traveled only by word of mouth or the printed page. The problem with word of mouth was that it could easily be altered, and the problem with the written word was that all copying was by hand, which made distribution a slow and tedious process.

Yet despite the primitive means of communication in ancient times, much significant communication took place. Scribes regularly recorded daily affairs, current events, and legal ongoings. Ancient archives have been and continue to be discovered throughout the ancient world that reveal information that complements the claims of the Bible.

In this chapter, we will investigate some of the known writings apart from the Bible that validate many of the historical facts of early Christianity and the life of Christ. These sources are divided into the following categories: secular Greco-Roman sources, non-Christian Jewish sources, and Christian sources.

According to professor Dr. Gary Habermas, there are 45 ancient, extrabiblical sources that reference the life of Christ, including:

- 19 creedal statements
- 4 archaeological sources (such as stones, graves, tablets)
- 17 non-Christian, secular writings
- 5 extrabiblical Christian sources (early church fathers)

Habermas says that "through this evidence we can substantiate 129 facts concerning the life, person, teachings, death, and resurrection of Jesus, plus the disciples' early message."[1]

Secular Non-Christian Sources

Thallus (c. 50–75)

Around A.D. 52, Thallus wrote a history of the Eastern Mediterranean world from the Trojan War to his time. Through the writings of Julius Africanus in 221, we read a reference from Thallus that discussed the darkness that occurred at the time of Jesus' death. He wrote:

> On the whole world there pressed a most fearful darkness; and the rocks were rent by an earthquake, and many places in Judea and other districts were thrown down. This darkness Thallus, in the third book of his History, calls, as appears to me without reason, an eclipse of the sun.[2]

In this brief statement, we find talk of the crucifixion, the spread of the gospel in the Mediterranean region in the middle of the first century, and a record that skeptics offered rationalistic explanations for certain Christian teachings and supernatural claims.

Pliny the Younger (c. 110)

Pliny was a Roman writer and administrator who served as the governor of Bithynia in Asia Minor (Turkey). He wrote about the persecution of the early Christians:

> They—the Christians—were in the habit of meeting on a certain fixed day before it was light, when they sang in alternate verses a hymn to Christ, as to a God, and bound themselves by a solemn oath, not to any wicked deeds, but never to commit any fraud, theft or adultery, never to falsify their word, nor deny a trust when they should be called upon to deliver it up; after which it was their custom to separate, and then reassemble to partake of food—but food of an ordinary and innocent kind.[3]

Pliny confirms those facts found in the New Testament books:

- Christ was worshiped as deity by the first generation of Christians.

- Jesus' ethical teachings were reflected in the oath taken by Christians never to be guilty of a number of sins mentioned in the letter.

- We find a probable reference to communion in Pliny's remark about Christians gathering to partake of ordinary food.

Tacitus (c. 115–120)

Cornelius Tacitus has been called the greatest historian of ancient Rome,[4] an individual generally acknowledged among scholars for his moral integrity. In his *Annals*, we find this entry:

> Consequently, to get rid of the report, Nero fastened the guilt and inflicted the most exquisite tortures on a class hated for their abominations, called Christians by the populace. Christus [Christ], from whom the name had

its origin, suffered the extreme penalty during the reign of Tiberius at the hands of one of our procurators, Pontius Pilate, and a most mischievous superstition [Christ's resurrection] thus checked for the moment, again broke out not only in Judea, the first source of the evil, but even in Rome, where all things hideous and shameful from every part of the world find their center and become popular.[5]

In this report we find six specific historical facts that agree with the New Testament:

1. Christians were named for their founder, *Christus* (Christ).

2. Christ was put to death by the Roman procurator Pontius Pilate.

3. This happened during the reign of Emperor Tiberius (between A.D. 14–37).

4. Christ's death ended the "superstition" (the resurrection) for a short time.

5. Christianity spread from Judea, from where it originated.

6. His followers carried this message to Rome.

Suetonius (c. 117–138)

Suetonius was chief secretary of Emperor Hadrian of Rome and had access to Imperial records. Writing about 115, he noted, "Because the Jews at Rome caused continuous disturbances *at the instigation of Chrestus [Christ],* he expelled them from the city."[6] In another place, he spoke regarding Christians and stated, "After the great fire at Rome...Punishments were also inflicted on *the Christians, a sect professing a new and mischievous religious belief.*"[7]

His account reveals three specific references to Christianity, including:

- It was Jesus who caused the Jews to make an uproar in Rome.

- Suetonius described Christianity's beliefs as mischievous—similar to how Tacitus records the concept of the resurrection.

- Suetonius specifically used the term *Christians,* referring to them as those who followed the teachings of Christ.

Lucian (c. 120–180)

A second-century Greek satirist, Lucian spoke with disdain toward early Christians. Yet even in doing so he confirmed some facts from the New Testament:

> The Christians, you know, worship a man to this day—the distinguished personage who introduced their novel rites, and was crucified on that account…and then it was impressed on them by their original law giver that they are all brothers, from the moment that they are converted, and deny the gods of Greece, and worshiped the crucified sage, and live after his laws.[8]

By the mid-second century, we find that even in this negative report, Christians worshipped a man named Jesus, a man who had been crucified. Upon conversion, these believers denied their former gods and followed Christ's teachings.

Galen (c. 150)

Galen was a famous physician of the second century. While his writings focus on medicine and the sciences, he includes four specific references to Christianity from Rome around 150, with the assumption that Christianity was already well known in the area by this time.[9]

Celsus (c. 170)[10]

In *Against Celsus,* the early church father Origen quotes Celsus, a second-century skeptic, on Jesus. Apparently the teachings of Celsus had become quite problematic, as Origen argues against 17 specific arguments from Celsus.[11]

Nearly every media source during this ancient time period comments on Jesus' existence or activities, indicating that Jesus at least lived as his friends claimed and operated in ways consistent with the secular sources.

What About *Earlier* Sources?

Yes, some of the writings mentioned here extend up to over a century after Jesus' death. We have to keep in mind that there are very few writings of any kind that still exist from the first century A.D. Wars, looting, fires, wear and tear, persecution, and even worms have destroyed many ancient scrolls and pages throughout the generations. It is interesting to note that according to more recent research, it has been observed that much of the Jewish and non-Jewish literature discovered up to A.D. 200 from the area where Jesus lived mentions Jesus or Christianity. This is exactly the *opposite* of what many have traditionally questioned—"If Jesus was so important, why didn't more ancient writers mention him?" The answer is, *they did.*

Jewish Sources

Jewish sources from the first two centuries of Christianity include the works of a famous Jewish historian named Josephus and a collection of rabbinical writings known as the Talmud.

Josephus (c. 37–97)

Josephus was born around the time Jesus died (A.D. 37) and wrote five major reference books, including a volume on the history of the Jews called *The Antiquities.* The English translation of his Greek masterpiece shares two significant sections on Jesus and Christianity. The shorter portion records:

[The high priest] convened the judges of the Sanhedrin, and brought before them the brother of Jesus, the one called Christ, whose name was James, and certain others, and accusing them of having transgressed the law delivered them up to be stoned.[12]

The reference here is clearly to James, brother of Jesus, who was put to death along with other Christians for their belief that Jesus was the Messiah. The New Testament makes reference to this in Acts 12.

When Peter escaped from jail, he shared with a group of believers, "Report these things to James and the brethren" (Acts 12:17 NASB).

Known as the leader of the first church in Jerusalem, James's death was a significant historical point for early Christianity—and apparently significant enough in secular culture to find a place in Josephus's account of Jewish history.

Josephus also mentions Jesus directly in one other place in *The Antiquities*. In an extended paragraph we find this:

Now there was about this time Jesus, a wise man, if it be lawful to call him a man; for he was a doer of wonderful works, a teacher of such men as receive the truth with pleasure. He drew over to him both many of the Jews and many of the Gentiles. He was [the] Christ. And when Pilate, at the suggestion of the principal men amongst us, had condemned him to the cross, those that loved him at the first did not forsake him; for he appeared to them alive again the third day; as the divine prophets had foretold these and ten thousand other wonderful things concerning him. And the tribe of Christians, so named from him, are not extinct to this day.

Some consider that the Christian references in this quote are later additions and should not be accepted as authentic. While there is question regarding the exact original Greek wording of this passage,

Shlomo Pines published a translation of a different version quoted in an Arabic manuscript of the tenth century. Its translation reads:

> At this time there was a wise man who was called Jesus, and his conduct was good, and he was known to be virtuous. And many people from among the Jews and the other nations became his disciples. Pilate condemned him to be crucified and to die. And those who had become his disciples did not abandon their loyalty to him. They reported that he had appeared to them three days after his crucifixion, and that he was alive. Accordingly they believed that he was the Messiah, concerning whom the Prophets have recounted wonders.

Pines suggests that this may be a more accurate record of what Josephus wrote, lacking the parts which have often been considered as later additions by Christian copyists. This would add weight to the argument that Josephus did write *something* about Jesus.

If this version is accurate, then the top Jewish historian of the first century made references to Jesus and reveals that Jesus was part of the cultural history of Palestine. He details (regardless of which of the above versions is accepted) that:

- Jesus was known as a wise man.
- He had many followers among Jews and Gentiles.
- Pilate condemned him to death by crucifixion.
- Jesus' followers reported that he was alive again.
- Christians claimed that Jesus had appeared on the third day after his crucifixion.
- Christians believed that Jesus was the Messiah mentioned by the Old Testament prophets.

The Talmud (compiled 70–200)

The Talmud was a collection of Jewish writings based on oral tradition extending back to the lifetime of Jesus. If you've read what the Jewish leaders claimed about Jesus in the Gospels, you already have a good idea of what the Talmud says about him. The Jewish leaders were not flattering and even accused Jesus of sorcery:

> ...on the eve of the Passover Yeshu [Jesus] was hanged [from the cross]. For forty days before the execution took place, a herald...cried, "He is going forth to be stoned because he has practiced sorcery and enticed Israel to apostasy."

This *Yeshu* was the Jewish name for Jesus. The word "hanging" is a symbolic reference to his execution, which the Gospel writers say came in the form of crucifixion. And the Jews had wanted to kill Jesus by stoning according to John 8:59, although they were not successful in this effort.

That Jewish writers in this time period—who were opposed to Jesus—would mention him in such ways only helps confirm that what Jesus' friends said about him was true.

Dr. Craig Blomberg, professor of New Testament studies at Denver Seminary, said this in an interview on *The John Ankerberg Show*:

> [The extrabiblical evidence for Jesus] may not seem like much until we realize that ancient historians for the most part centered only on the lives and exploits of kings, of generals, of religious leaders in institutional positions of power, and that Jesus held none of these powerful roles. In fact, it is only to the extent that he comes in contact with Herod or Pilate or the various ruling families that mention is made of him [in secular non-Christian sources]. From that point of view it is remarkable that we have any references to him at all in a period of time when people did not know the movement that would grow to universal proportions. But we certainly have enough to know that he lived and to confirm the basic outline of the life of Christ from the Gospels.[13]

Christian Sources

Outside of the New Testament documents, of which several thousand early manuscript copies exist, a number of additional early Christian writings share information about Jesus and the early activities of his followers. The second generation of Christianity includes eight specific sources supporting the original stories by Jesus' friends.[14] These were written by early church fathers, or second- and third-generation believers of Christ's original followers. In addition to spreading the teachings as taught directly from the apostles, they help affirm the acceptance and accuracy of the New Testament text from frequent references in their writings. For instance, Irenaeus (A.D. 170) quoted 23 of the 27 New Testament books less than 100 years after their writing, meaning he had access to these books *together* within a generation of the apostles. This would have been a tremendous accomplishment for a culture whose writings could be spread only through handwritten copies!

Clement (writing c. 95)

The earliest of these Christian sources was Clement, a leader in the church at Rome. In his letter to the Corinthian church around A.D. 95, he cites portions of Matthew, Mark, and Luke, where he introduces them as the actual words of Jesus.

Clement lived in Rome in the years immediately following the deaths of the apostles Peter and Paul. He led a Christian church there and continued to communicate that the same Jesus the apostles had been killed for had lived, died, and risen from the dead. Clement also wrote that the accounts handed down in the Gospels by Jesus' friends were true.

The Didache (50–160)

Perhaps the second earliest Christian writing available outside of the New Testament authors was a document called the Didache ("The Teachings"). This document served as an ancient manual of

Christianity that dates between the end of the first century to the beginning of the second. It cites portions of the first three Gospels, referring to them as the words of Jesus, with extensive quotes from Matthew.

Papias (writing c. 125–140)

Among other early Christian sources are the works of an early church leader named Papias. He served as a pastor at the church in Hierapolis, a town six miles north of Laodicea (on the Lycus River in modern-day western Turkey). It was a church founded as a result of Paul's missionary work,[15] and the church was traditionally believed to be led by the same Philip mentioned in Acts 6. The church continued to grow despite persecution through the early second century.

Papias circulated a collection of his sermons, titled the *Exposition of Oracles of the Lord,* around A.D. 130, in which he mentioned Matthew, Mark, Luke, and John as accepted and authentic works. He specifically referred to John's Gospel as containing the words of Jesus. For those seeking to discredit early Christianity, it is difficult to argue against the fact that a second-generation Christian was quoting all four Gospels less than 100 years after the life of Jesus. Within about 35 years of the authorship of John's Gospel, Papias was quoting John's words from a church in western Turkey.

Papias said that he felt compelled to learn directly from those who had personally lived and served alongside the apostles of Jesus. Through the early church historian Eusebius we read these words from Papias:

> If I met with any one who had been a follower of the elders anywhere, I made it a point to inquire what were the declarations of the elders; what was said by Andrew, Peter, or Philip; what by Thomas, James, John, Matthew, or any other of the disciples of our Lord; what was said by Aristion and the presbyter John, disciples of the Lord. For I do not

think that I derived so much benefit from books as from the living voice of those that are still surviving.

Justin Martyr (100–165)

In the mid-second century, we find an additional extrabiblical source written by Justin Martyr, known as the best defender of Christianity during his era (A.D. 140). He considered all four Gospels to be accurate and communicated among the Roman culture of his time. Justin Martyr quoted from the apostle John in Ephesus (modern-day Turkey) only a generation after the original text was written. This complements modern research that had dated a parchment scrap of John's Gospel to as early as A.D. 125. In *I Apologies* 61.4, Justin Martyr wrote, "Christ also said 'Unless you are born again you will not enter into the kingdom of heaven.'"

Polycarp (69–155)

Polycarp, a student of the apostle John, also quotes portions of Matthew, Mark, and Luke, referring to them as the very words of Jesus around A.D. 150.

Polycarp is among other early church fathers who considered Jesus as God from the time of the apostles. Some of the others include:

- *Clement* (A.D. 95) called Jesus "the high priest of our offerings, the guardian and helper of our weaknesses... for he, being the radiance of his majesty, is as much superior to angels as the name he has inherited is more excellent."[16]

- *2 Clement* (A.D. 180) noted that "we ought to think of Jesus Christ, as we do of God, as Judge of the living and the dead."

- *Ignatius* (A.D. 110) called Jesus "born and unborn, God in man" and "son of man and son of God."[17]

- *Melito of Sardis* (A.D. 160) in his *Discourse on the Cross,* said that Christians affirmed both the humanity and the divinity of Jesus side by side.

Irenaeus (120–202)

Irenaeus, a student of Polycarp, quoted from 23 of the 27 New Testament books by A.D. 170, omitting only the shortest books, such as Philemon and 3 John.

The Muratorian Fragment (c. 174)

By the last quarter of the second century, we discover two further Christian sources, including the Muratorian Fragment from A.D. 174, which lists Matthew, Mark, Luke, and John as the four Gospels. In total, this list includes 23 of the 27 New Testament books.

Papyrus 45 (c. 200)

Finally, scholars have dated what they call Papyrus 45 at around A.D. 200. This remnant mentions all four Gospels together and labels them as authentic writings by the followers of Jesus.

What Does This Mean?

We can see from many sources that Jesus and key events found in the Bible were mentioned by other ancient writers in ways that correspond with and complement the biblical accounts. The Bible cannot be proven true by observing these extrabiblical writings, but the abundance of materials that agree with the biblical accounts points toward the Bible's accuracy at a level far beyond that of any other source of ancient writing. The extrabiblical evidence is substantial enough that it cannot be taken lightly. It builds a very powerful case for the authenticity and reliability of the Bible.

THE SCIENCE OF THE BIBLE:
Can Science and Scripture Complement One Another?

There are many people today who believe that science and the Bible are incompatible. And there are some who claim that the facts of science prove the Bible wrong.

While the Bible is not a science textbook, when it comes to science, it is accurate, and this accuracy stands as a powerful testimony to its divine nature. As Dr. Norman Geisler has noted, "Given that not much scientific information was known in Bible times, the Bible speaks with considerable scientific credibility, an evidence of its supernatural nature."[1]

Scientists themselves have frequently been impressed by the scientific accuracy of the Bible. Dr. Hugh Ross recalls his thoughts when he first investigated the Bible as an unbeliever while he was testing various sacred books for scientific and historical accuracy:

> I found the Bible noticeably different. It was simple, direct, and specific. I was amazed at the quantity of historical and scientific (testable) material it included and at the detail of this material...For the next year and a half I spent about an hour a day searching the Bible for scientific and historical inaccuracies. I finally had to admit that it was error free and that this perfect accuracy could only come from the Creator Himself...Further, I had proven to myself, on the basis of predicted history and science, that the Bible was

more reliable than many of the laws of physics. My only rational option was to trust the Bible's authority to the same degree as I trusted the laws of physics.[2]

Mark Eastman and Chuck Missler, authors of *The Creator Beyond Time and Space,* provide in their book a number of examples that illustrate how the Bible was thousands of years ahead of its time on issues of science. They write,

> There are dozens of passages in the Bible which demonstrate tremendous scientific foreknowledge...We find that the scientific statements in the Bible are without error or contradiction...When the biblical text is carefully examined the reader will quickly discover an uncanny scientific accuracy unparalleled by any document of antiquity...the Bible does describe scientific phenomena in common terminology with unmistakable clarity...In virtually all ancient religious documents it is common to find scientifically inaccurate myths about the nature of the universe and the life forms on planet earth. Any cursory review of ancient mythology will readily confirm this statement. However, the Bible is unique because of the conspicuous absence of such myths. In fact, throughout the Bible we find scientifically accurate concepts about the physical universe that were not "discovered" by modern scientists until very recent times.[3]

Among the examples they cite are these:

- Psalm 102:25-26, Isaiah 51:6, Matthew 24:35: Heaven and earth will pass away.

- Jeremiah 33:22: The stars of the heavens cannot be numbered. Scientists did not believe the number of stars could be determined until recently. There are now at least 100 billion trillion—a number no one could count.

- Psalm 19:6: The sun follows a circular path. Modern science has shown this is accurate.

- Job 36:27-28: Mentions the earth's hydrological cycle centuries before the process was known to scientists.

Facts of Science and the Bible

The Bible contains many specific scientific facts that have been affirmed in modern science. That these facts are noted repeatedly in the Bible thousands of years before their modern discovery points to the accuracy of the Bible in matters of science. That the Bible does so without error points to the Bible as a source of supernatural information, or what Christians call divine revelation. Here are some of the facts:

Key Aspects of Creation

The first three verses of Genesis accurately state all known aspects of the created universe (Genesis 1:1-3). Science defines the universe in terms of time, space, matter, and energy. In Genesis 1:1,3 we find these same elements: "In the beginning [time] God created the heavens [space] and the earth [matter]...And God said, 'Let there be light [energy].'" No other creation account agrees with the observable evidence.[4]

The Earth's Foundations

Over a thousand years before the New Testament was written, the Hindu scriptures recorded that the earth sat upon the backs of several large elephants who rested on the back of a very large turtle who swam in a sea. According to Greek mythology, Atlas held the earth on his shoulders. But the Old Testament book of Job says, "He suspends the earth over nothing" (Job 26:7). According to one of the earliest Old Testament books, the earth is suspended in space. Nothing is holding it up. Job wrote about the same time the Hindu scriptures were written. How did Job know this scientific fact? Only God could have revealed this information to Job.

The Shape of the Earth

All through ancient times till a few hundred years ago, humans believed the earth was flat. They thought that if a person sailed too far, he or she would fall over the edge. It was not until the 1500s that this idea was proven inaccurate. However, many hundreds of years earlier, the prophet Isaiah wrote, "He sits enthroned above the circle of the earth, and its people are like grasshoppers. He stretches out the heavens like a canopy, and spreads them out like a tent to live in" (Isaiah 40:22).

Over 2500 years ago the Bible described the earth as a sphere, saying that the skies ("heavens") are spread out like a tent.

The Valleys of the Sea

Without the help of submarines or underwater sonar, the Bible discussed in detail how the bottom of the oceans and seas look. In Psalm 18:15, written around 1000 B.C., we read about the "valleys of the sea." Ancient people did not know what lay hidden underwater. How could Psalm 18:15 accurately describe the ocean's bottom? Again, the evidence points toward the divine revelation of God.

Global Wind Patterns

Not until the invention of modern satellite technology did scientists understand the wind patterns that circle our globe. Yet in the Old Testament book of Ecclesiastes, written around 1000 B.C., we find this: "The wind blows to the south and turns to the north; round and round it goes, ever returning on its course" (1:6). Again, for a writer to document this information 3000 years ago points toward an external, divine source of revelation, just as the Bible claims.[5]

Lightning, Thunder, and Rain

In ancient times, most religious writings taught that lightning bolts were missiles thrown in anger by various gods. In China, Taoist scripture regarded the rainbow as a deadly rain dragon. In Confu-cian scripture, the goddess of lightning, Tien Mu, flashed light on intended victims to enable Lei Kung, the god of thunder, to launch his deadly bolts accurately.[6]

In contrast, the Bible provides an accurate statement about light-ning and rain. Job 28:26 notes that God "made a decree for the rain and a path for the thunderstorm." What's more, in Job 36:27-28 we find a very precise description of the hydrological cycle, in which water evaporates into the air, and comes down as rain. It was not until the late 1600s that the scientists Perrault, Mariotte, and Halley scientifically affirmed this water cycle.

The Weight of the Wind

Ancient cultures believed that air was weightless. Not until 1643 did the Italian scientist Torricelli discover barometric pressure.[7] Yet in the book of Job we read, "When He imparted weight to the wind and meted out the waters by measure..." (Job 28:25 NASB). The Bible spoke of air's weight thousands of years before science did. Again, the source of this revelation? God himself, according to the Bible.

Spreading of Disease

According to an article from The Way of the Master,[8] Encyclo-pedia Britannica documents that in 1845, a young doctor in Vienna named Dr. Ignaz Semmelweis was horrified at the terrible death rate of women who gave birth in hospitals. As many as 30 percent died after giving birth. Semmelweis noted that doctors in these hospitals would perform autopsies on patients who had died, then, without washing their hands, would go straight to another ward to examine expectant mothers. This was their normal practice because the pres-ence of microscopic diseases was unknown. Semmelweis insisted that doctors wash their hands before examinations, and the death rate immediately dropped to two percent.

The necessity of washing hands to protect from the spread of infectious diseases coincides with the specific instructions God gave the Jewish people for when they encountered disease: "When a man is cleansed from discharge, he is to count off seven days for his ceremonial cleansing; he must wash his clothes and bathe himself with fresh water, and he will be clean" (Leviticus 15:13). Until recent years, doctors washed their hands in a bowl of water, which still left invisible germs on their hands. However, the Bible requires that hands be washed under "running water" (Leviticus 15:13 NASB). The fact that this information was known by Moses and the early Israelites in ancient times as part of God's law is stunning.

The First and Second Laws of Thermodynamics

The First Law of Thermodynamics states that matter can be neither created nor destroyed, and that the amount of matter in the universe remains constant. If the First Law is correct, then the universe could not have created itself. It must have been created in the past, no further creating must be going on, and no loss of creation is occurring. The Bible correctly portrays this law in its creation account (Genesis 1–2) and in Hebrews 1:3, which mentions God's sustaining power in holding creation together.

The Second Law of Thermodynamics states that all systems degenerate from order to disorder. Albert Einstein regarded this as a key law in science. The Bible agrees with this law when it notes that "the earth will wear out like a garment and its inhabitants die like flies" (Isaiah 51:6).[9]

Crop Rotation

Agricultural experts have come to realize the importance of allowing farm lands a period of rest approximately every seven years to allow for the replenishment of nutrients in the soil. Yet the Bible stated the necessity of crop rotation back in the time of Moses, in approximately 1450 B.C. Leviticus 25:4-5 notes, "In the seventh year the land is to have a sabbath of rest, a sabbath to the LORD. Do not sow your fields or prune your vineyards. Do not reap what grows of itself or harvest the grapes of your untended vines. The land is to have a year of rest."[10]

Scientists and the Bible

Many scientists throughout history have viewed the Bible as the divine Word of God. They have stated that science and the Bible are not in conflict. In my (John's) book with John Weldon, *Fast Facts on Defending Your Faith*, we list the following 25 scientific experts who also embraced the truth of Scripture:[11]

1. Johannes Kepler (1571–1630), founder of physical astronomy

2. Robert Boyle (1627–1691), father of modern chemistry

3. Blaise Pascal (1623–1662), an early great mathematician who laid the foundations for areas of study such as hydrodynamics, differential calculus, and probability theory

4. John Ray (1627–1705), father of English natural history and probably the best zoologist and botanist of his time

5. Nicolaus Steno (1631–1686), father of stratigraphy (study of rock layers in geology)

6. William Petty (1623–1687) helped institute the science of statistics and the modern study of economics

7. Isaac Newton (1642–1727) invented calculus, discovered the law of gravity and the three laws of motion, developed the particle theory of light propagation, and invented the reflecting telescope

8. Carolus Linnaeus (1707–1778), father of biological taxonomy

9. Michael Faraday (1791–1867), one of the world's greatest physicists, developed essential concepts in electricity and

    magnetism, invented the electrical generator, and made numerous contributions to chemistry

10. Georges Cuvier (1769–1832), founder of comparative anatomy

11. Charles Babbage (1792–1871), founder of computer science

12. John Dalton (1766–1844), father of atomic theory

13. Matthew Maury (1806–1873), founder of oceanography

14. James Simpson (1811–1879) discovered the anesthetic properties of chloroform and introduced its use in medicine

15. James Joule (1818–1889) discovered the mechanical equivalent of heat, laying the foundation for the study of thermodynamics

16. Louis Agassiz (1807–1873), father of glacial geology

17. Gregor Mendel (1822–1884), father of genetics

18. Louis Pasteur (1822–1895), father of bacteriology

19. Joseph Lister (1827–1912), founder of antiseptic surgical methods

20. William Thomson, Lord Kelvin (1824–1907), one of the greatest physicists who established thermodynamics on a formal scientific basis, supplying a strict statement of the first two laws of thermodynamics

21. Joseph Clerk Maxwell (1831–1879) created a systematic theoretical and mathematical framework for electromagnetic field theory—Einstein praised Maxwell's contributions as the best in physics since Newton

22. Bernhard Riemann (1826–1866), developer of non-Euclidian geometry, used by Einstein in his development of relativity theory

23. Joseph Henry Gilbert (1817–1901) developed nitrogen

and superphosphate fertilizers for farm crops and code-
veloped the first agricultural experimental station, laying
a foundation for advances in agricultural science that
enabled farmers to feed millions

24. John Ambrose Fleming (1849–1945) invented the
Fleming valve, laying the foundation for ensuing devel-
opments in electronics

25. Wernher Von Braun (1912–1977), father of space
science

The Scientific Laws of Nature[12]

How did the laws of nature come to be? Who authored them?
These questions have been asked since ancient times by many.
The laws that govern our cosmos appear to be changeless. They
have operated from the first moments of creation until the present
moment.

The speed of light, for instance, is finite (299.793 km/s) and
changeless as it travels through the medium of space. Stars that
formed at many different distances from us, and in many different
time frames, could not have come into existence had the laws of
physics, such as the constant speed of light, been variable. Because
we know both the speed of light and the distances to faraway stars,
we can calculate their age with the help of a simple formula. This
enables us to determine the age of the universe.

There are four fundamental forces in nature that not only have
precise values, but are also changeless. These are the (1) electromagnetic, (2) gravitational, (3) strong nuclear, and (4) weak nuclear
forces. Even slight variations in any of these forces, or a variation
in light speed, would make life impossible. There are many other
examples of physical constants that must have precise, changeless
value both in the past and present. Even skeptics and adherents
of naturalism who deny the existence of the supernatural sometimes express awe at nature's orderliness and coherence. They enjoy

the world of nature. However, they do not express any particular surprise at the precision and constancy of nature's physical laws. Worse, they cry "Unreasonable! Irrational! Illogical!" at those who believe effects have causes, that design points to a designer, or that order and beauty do not evolve from chaos. Who, then, has a better grip on reason, rationality, and logic?

The four fundamental forces permit elements and atoms to exist and hold together, and allow the formation of thousands of chemically bonded compounds. Every bit of matter we encounter every day of our lives holds together because of the existence and precise value of the four fundamental forces. Without these forces there would be nothing but a chaotic sea of particles. Perhaps the apostle Paul was not a sophisticated scientist, but through him we are given this powerful insight in Colossians 1:16-17:

> By him all things were created: things in heaven and on earth, visible and invisible, whether thrones or powers or rulers or authorities; all things were created by him and for him. He is before all things, and in him all things hold together.

At the beginning of this chapter we pointed out that the Bible is not a science textbook and should not be treated as such. However, where the Bible does speak on issues of science, it provides accurate descriptions that were given centuries before they were affirmed by scientists. As Eastman and Missler conclude:

> To argue that the evidences for biblical inspiration are the result of a myriad of lucky guesses requires an enormous measure of faith. Such an assertion requires us to believe that ancient fishermen, tent makers, shepherds, kings and paupers, who were separated by 1500 years on three different continents, could consistently, and without error, describe the nature of the universe, planet Earth and its life forms, in a way that is fully consistent with twentieth-century science. It requires us to believe that those same

men wrote history in advance—all of this without the guidance of One with supernatural "inside information."[13]

Such scientific accuracy makes the Bible not only unique, it makes the Bible supernatural. The Bible is accurate historically and scientifically. As a result, we can also trust it to provide reliable information on matters of salvation, eternity, and our daily spiritual lives.

9

I
n earlier chapters, we stated that the Bible is inspired and that the original text was perfect. In addition, we have shown that with the help of many early manuscript copies, the historical accuracy of the Bible we have today is over 99 percent accurate from the original manuscript. But what about the whole matter of translating the Bible from its original languages to English?

Due to its amazing influence, a strong movement persists that argues that *only* the King James Version of the Bible is accurate and should be used by English readers today. In this chapter, we'll discuss the key issues in this debate.

Key Issues in the King James-Only Debate

Some Christians today believe that the King James Version (KJV) of the Bible is the only legitimate and trustworthy English-translation Bible. Further, like the original writings of Scripture, they believe that only the KJV is inspired and inerrant (without error).

There are several distinct KJV groups: 1) people who prefer the KJV above all other Bibles but are not KJV only; 2) people who argue that the underlying Hebrew and Greek texts used by the KJV translators are superior to all other texts. This group would not necessarily argue that such texts are inspired but that they more accurately reflect the original writings; 3) those who argue that only the Textus

Receptus (TR) has been supernaturally preserved and inspired and is therefore inerrant (the TR is the text on which the KJV was based; there are over 30 editions, none 100 percent identical). For those who hold this view, the KJV translation itself would not necessarily be inspired; 4) those who argue that the KJV translation itself constitutes an inspired and inerrant text. This is the most dominant of the four groups, and categories three and four comprise the core of the controversy and are our principal concern here.

Sadly the King James-only controversy is an issue largely based on inaccurate arguments. However, it is a topic Christians have been forced to address. Why? This issue has fueled the division of churches, ministries, and other groups over the past century.

The majority of perceived problems raised by the development of new Bible translations arise from two sources: 1) from misconceptions about the KJV, and 2) from a lack of understanding regarding the origin and transmission of the Bible (including the nature of translation work and the textual data we possess).

The degree of uncertainty raised by textual questions (what is actually in the manuscripts) is far less than the degree of uncertainty raised by how we interpret what the manuscripts say. In other words, even when the text is certain, there is often an honest difference of opinion among interpreters regarding the precise meaning of the verses.

In essence, the King James-only debate concerns three basic issues: 1) evaluating the "families" of manuscripts (deciding whether the minority of earliest manuscripts or the majority of late manuscripts are closer to the originals); 2) determining the best text from among all the manuscripts we possess (this concerns the one to two percent relevant variant readings found when comparing manuscripts); and 3) producing a good translation—accurately translating the Hebrew, Aramaic, and Greek words in the manuscripts. It also includes the methods brought to the translating process (whether the members of the translation committees translated words properly and the degree to which they sacrificed a strict literal translation in order to translate the meaning more accurately to fit the contemporary language in use today and by doing so enhance the understanding of Scripture).

The first two points involve what are referred to as *textual variants*, or differences among the early copies of the Bible. An example of a textual variant can be found in John 6:47, where the KJV reads, "He that believeth *on me* hath everlasting life" (emphasis added). Modern translations read, "He who believes has eternal life"—the words "on me" are not included. The reason they are not present is because they are not found in the earliest manuscripts. Contextually, the meaning is exactly the same even if the words "on me" are not in the verse. In the immediate and larger contexts, it is clear that the term "on me" is implied. So this kind of textual variant does not change the meaning.

An example of a *translational difference* can be found in John 3:36, where the KJV reads, "He that *believeth not* the Son shall not see life," whereas the New American Standard Bible (NASB) reads, "He who *does not obey* the Son will not see life" (emphases added). Are we dealing with unbelief or disobedience? Are there any implications here for the doctrine of salvation by grace through faith alone? At issue is how to properly translate the single Greek word *apeitheo* that is found in John 3:36. This term can be translated as either "unbelief" or "disobedience." To illustrate, the KJV translates the same word, *apeitheo*, as "disobedience" in other places, such as 1 Peter 3:1 ("obey not"); 4:17 ("obey not"); and Romans 2:8 ("do not obey").

The main reason contemporary translations translate the Greek term as "disobey" is because this is the primary meaning of the term. Most words have multiple meanings, but usually one is primary or the most common meaning. The KJV translation of "disbelief" is a secondary translation by extension—it is not the direct, primary translation. The KJV is not mistranslating the term because it *is* a possible translation. But the KJV is not giving the most literal usage.[1] Regardless, this is not a major issue, as King James-only proponents argue that "there is no conflict between obedience to Christ and belief in Christ. True faith is obedience to Christ" because a "disobedient faith" is a nonentity. "Just because there are those who might misuse the term 'obey' so as to promote a works-salvation viewpoint does not in any way change the meaning of the term itself."[2]

A Quick History of the King James Version

Many King James-only writers argue God had the KJV written so that, through the translators, he could produce a perfect English Bible. However, the reality is that it was written for a far more practical reason: to produce a good standard translation that would be most acceptable to all concerned. Understanding the background of the KJV helps us comprehend the issues involved.

How did we get the KJV? The KJV Bible was first published in 1611. Subsequent printings or editions corrected a number of translation errors (in 1612, 1613, 1616, 1629, 1638, 1660, 1683, 1727, 1762, 1769, and 1873). Each of these versions differed in certain places from the previous edition. There were even two slightly different 1611 editions and six slightly different editions in the 1650s.

There are even a few *significant* differences between the 1611 edition and our modern version. For example, in 1611, the KJV had "Then cometh Judas" in Matthew 26:36. Today it is rendered in the KJV as "Then cometh Jesus." This is a rather significant change.

There have also been a few embarrassing printing errors. The 1631 printing omitted the word "not" from the seventh commandment, inadvertently encouraging people to commit adultery. This King James edition became known as the Wicked Bible. Another printing of the KJV became known as the Unrighteous Bible because it stated that the *unrighteous* will inherit the kingdom of heaven. And a few printing errors continue to occur in the KJV and other versions today.[3]

The KJV Bible we use today is based primarily on a major revision completed in 1769. This was 158 years after the first edition. If the 1611 edition is the true Word of God, as some have claimed, it is no longer in use. And if it's not, then which KJV edition do King James-only writers claim is God's perfect Word or translation?

In making the New Testament translation, the King James translators used the 1516 Greek text of the Catholic scholar Desiderius Erasmus. Erasmus took less than a year to produce his text, which was based on portions of only five or six late manuscripts from the twelfth to fourteenth centuries. In addition, he produced his work quickly in order to be the first to publish a Greek New Testament (the printing press was still relatively new at this point in history). Not surprisingly, given the conditions under which Erasmus worked, the various editions of his text contain numerous corrections. Both Stephanus and Beza revised his text. It is this Greek text, along with Erasmus' *Complutensian Polyglot,* that was used by the translators to produce the first edition of the King James Bible (1611).

Some of the problems Erasmus bypassed in his hasty work have been summarized by noted Princeton scholar Bruce M. Metzger:

> For most of the text he relied on two rather inferior manuscripts in the university library at Basle, one of the Gospels and one of the Acts and Epistles, both dating from about the twelfth century...[Because of back translation from Latin into Greek in a manuscript of Revelation] here and there...are readings which have never been found in any known Greek manuscript but which are still perpetuated today in printings of the so-called Textus Receptus of the Greek New Testament.

> Evidence like this demonstrates that Erasmus' text, which evolved and became the basis for the Textus Receptus, "...was not based on early manuscripts, not reliably edited, and consequently not trustworthy."[4]

It was not until 1624 that the Elzevir brothers published their edition. In the second edition (1633) the preface claimed that it was the text "best received of all." This "received text," known as the Textus Receptus, is the text behind the KJV New Testament. It differs from the Erasmus text in only a few hundred minor instances. In spite of Erasmus' use of only five or six relatively late manuscripts, the changes made in all KJV editions were minor. For example, in the nineteenth century the American Bible Society examined six KJV editions then circulating. Of the 24,000 variants (the great majority in punctuation and some of the text), it noted, "of the great number, there is not one which mars the integrity of the text or affects any doctrine or precept of the Bible."[5] This is because the King James translators had used the same basic principles employed by modern translators, and their skill and scholarship gave us what became the standard English Bible for 400 years.

Typos in the History of the English Bible

1. One of the Ten Commandments stated "Thou shalt commit adultery" in a 1631 edition of the King James Bible.

2. The Camel's Bible of 1823 took that nickname from a misprint in Genesis 24:61, which read, "And Rebekah arose, and her camels" instead of "her damsels."

3. A Bible printed in Oxford, England, in 1792 has been dubbed the Denial Bible. In this Bible, Philip is said to be the disciple who denied Jesus in Luke 22:35, rather than Peter.

4. A couple of rather glaring mistakes can be found in a Bible produced in 1807. Matthew 13:43, instead of saying, "Who hath ears to hear," says, "Who hath ears to ears."

5. The same 1807 Bible has Hebrews 9:14 declaring, "How much more shall the blood of Christ...purge your conscience from good works [should be 'dead works'] to serve the living God."

6. Produced during the reign of King Charles I in the 1600s, Psalm 14:1 reads, "The fool hath said in his heart, There is a God."

7. In the 1970 first edition of the King James II New Testament, John 1:5 reads, "And the light shines in the darkness, and the darkness overcomes it."

8. The Unrighteous Bible of 1653 said, "Know ye not that the unrighteous shall inherit the kingdom of God" (1 Corinthians 6:9).
—From: http://www.biblecollectors.org/bible_misprints.htm

The King James Translators on the King James Version

King James-only proponents argue that the 1611 edition of the King James Bible is the most accurate because it is divinely inspired and therefore inerrant. Some have even argued it should be used to correct the Greek and Hebrew manuscripts we now possess.

However, if we examine what the KJV translators stated about their translation, the proof rests entirely *against* this position. The translators made no claims for divine inspiration in producing their translation. Instead, they candidly admitted their translation was imperfect. What exactly did the King James translators say?

The translators began their preface to the reader by noting their expectation that their translation would come under unfair criticism and attack, just as the church father Jerome was criticized when he translated the Bible into Latin in the fourth century. The translators regretfully stated that their attempt to provide a new and accurate translation of the Scriptures into the common English tongue will be "welcomed with suspicion instead of love, and with emulation instead of thanks: and if there be any hole left for cavil to enter... it is sure to be misconstrued, and in danger to be condemned" (p. 1, 1611 preface).

They wanted Scripture to be known and understood. As the translators themselves noted, the Word of God had been hidden from the people by the policies of the Roman Catholic Church, and there was a genuine need for a new translation in the common language. The translators wrote,

> We shall be traduced by Popish persons at home or abroad, who therefore will malign us, because we are poor instruments to make God's holy Truth to be yet more and more

known unto the people, whom they desire still to keep in ignorance and darkness (p. ii).

...happy is the man that delighteth in the Scripture and thrice happy that meditate in it day and night. But how shall man meditate in that which they cannot understand? How shall they understand that which is kept close [veiled] in an unknown tongue?...[contemporary] translation it is that opens the window, to let in the light...indeed, without translation into the vulgar [common] tongue, the unlearned are but like children at Jacob's well (which was deep) without a bucket or something to draw with... (pp. 3-4).

Other quotes from the 1611 preface note the translators' intentions to create a quality English translation while not claiming their work was perfect:

Truly (good Christian reader) we never thought from the beginning, that we should need to make a new Translation, nor yet to make of a bad one a good one...But to make a good one better, or out of many good ones, one principal good one...that has been our endeavor (p. 9).

Some per adventure would have no variety of senses to be set in the margin, lest the authority of the Scriptures for deciding of controversies by that show of uncertainty should somewhat be shaken. But we hold their judgment not to be so sound in this point (p. 10).

Since the King James translators did not have a vast number of manuscript copies at their disposal for comparison's sake and research tools were limited, the precise meanings of words that occurred only once or twice in the Scriptures were sometimes unknown and difficult to translate. They said,

It has pleased God in his divine providence, here and there to scatter words and sentences of [a particular] difficulty and doubtfulness, not in doctrinal points that concern salva-tion…but in matters of less moment…There be many words in the scriptures, which be never found there but once…so that we cannot be helped by conference of places. Again, there be many rare names of certain birds, beasts and pre-cious stones, etc. concerning which the Hebrews themselves are so divided among themselves for judgment…Now in such a case, does not a margin do well to admonish the Reader to seek further, and not to conclude or dogmatize upon this or that peremptorily?…[T]o determine of such things as the Spirit of God has left…questionable, can be no less than presumption.

Therefore, as St. Augustine said, that variety of Translations is profitable for the finding out of the sense of the Scrip-tures: so diversity of signification and sense in the margin, where the text is not so clear, must need do good, yea, is necessary, as we are persuaded (p. 10).

Note that the translators said a *variety* of translations is profit-able for understanding Scriptures.

Is the King James Version Inspired?

As noted, most King James-only proponents claim that the KJV is perfect and without error. Dr. Samuel C. Gipp says of the 1611 KJV, "I believe the *King James Bible* is perfect" and Peter Ruckman even thinks "[so-called] Mistakes in the A.V. 1611 are advanced revelation!"[6] Most King James-only adherents also believe the KJV is divinely inspired. The difficulty with such a view is that the KJV has clear errors. This leaves only two options: either the KJO posi-tion is wrong, or God has inspired errors in his Word.

But advocates usually claim that anyone who criticizes the KJV is "against God and his Word." However, we have noted that even the KJV translators criticized their own translation by their subsequent corrections. In other words, to point out errors in the KJV should not be considered an attack on the Word of God but a correction in translation. Again, the KJV translators' alternate renderings in the margins of their Bible pages prove they did not believe their translation was inerrant.

Errors in the King James Version

There are not a large number of errors in the KJV, but they do exist, which should not be surprising considering the translation work was done 400 years ago. For example, in Psalm 12:7 the translation "Thou shalt keep *them*" should be "Thou shalt keep *us*." Contextually and grammatically the pronoun should refer to people, not words. Ninety-five percent of Hebrew scholars agree the KJV has made an error here.[7] In Isaiah 4:5 "canopy" is mistranslated as "defence"; in Isaiah 5:25 "refuse" is mistranslated as "torn"; in Acts 19:2 "when" is translated as "since."

Theologian James White points out some other translation errors in the KJV:

- Mark 6:20—"observed" should be "kept him safe" or "protected"

- Acts 5:30—"and" should be "by"

- James 3:2—"we offend all" should be "in many ways"

- 1 Corinthians 4:4—"For I know nothing by myself" should be "For I am conscious of nothing against myself"

- Isaiah 65:11—"that troop" and "unto that number" should be the literal Hebrew "Gad" and "Mani"; these are translated in modern versions as "fortune" and "destiny" because Gad and Mani were the Babylonian or Assyrian gods, the God of Fortune (Gad) and the God of Destiny (Mani)

- 1 Kings 10:28—"linen yarn" should be the town of Kue in Egypt

- 1 Chronicles 5:26—the second use of the term "and" should be "even"[8]

White also points out that KJV mistranslation is responsible for a number of seeming contradictions in the Bible (frequently pointed out by skeptics) that do not actually exist in the original Greek text (such as Acts 9:7 with 22:9).[9]

Further, names are also problematic in the KJV because the translators sometimes used a Greek form, a Latin form, or the Hebrew form of a name. For example, *Jesus* and *Joshua* are both names given to the same Old Testament character (Acts 7:45; Hebrews 4:8). Different spellings for the same person include Cis and Kish; Noe and Noah; Kora and Core; Hosea and Osee; Isaiah and Esay; Judas, Judah, Juda, and Jude; Zera and Zarah.

In addition, the KJV, as the translators admitted, used a large number of ways to translate the same word:

> It is universally agreed that by their variety [of translating the same word] the translators confuse the reader...[For example] *dabhar* ("a word" or "thing") is rendered by eighty-four separate English words, *panim* ("face") by thirty-four, *sim* ("to set" or "place") by fifty-nine...*nasah* ("to lift up") by forty-six, *abhar* ("to pass over") by forty-eight, *rabh* ("much" or "many") by forty-four, and *tobh* ("good") by forty-one. Similar variety is seen in the New Testament, where *katargein* ("to make void") appears twenty-seven times and is rendered seventeen different ways...[10]

Other examples include the Hebrew term for "turn back" (in a single grammatical form) being rendered by 60 different words. In Acts 12:4, the Hebrew word for passover is actually translated "Easter" even though in every other place it is translated "passover" by the KJV, some 28 times.[11]

There are also a number of KJV translations in which the wording is confusing. For example, "And mount Sinai was altogether on a smoke" (Exodus 19:18); "Thou shalt destroy them that speak leasing"

(Psalm 5:6); "The ships of Tarshish did sing of thee in thy market" (Ezekiel 27:25); and, "We do you to wit of the grace of God" (2 Corinthians 8:1).

Here are some examples of KJV errors that haven't been corrected:

- "my sore ran in the night" (Psalm 77:2) should be "my hand was stretched out"
- "pineth away" (Mark 9:18) should be "becomes rigid"
- "touch me not" (John 20:17) should be "do not keep on holding me"
- "abstain from all appearance of evil" (1 Thessalonians 5:22) should be "every form of evil"

None of this implies the KJV is not a good and accurate translation; it only demonstrates that the KJV translators, great scholars that they were, were still imperfect and made some errors. It also highlights the logical inconsistencies of those who argue for a King James-only position.

Let's Be Thankful

Both King James-only promoters and those who use modern translations have been more than blessed by God as far as his Word is concerned. We are privileged to have the Word of God more complete than the vast majority of God's people throughout history. Abraham and his family did not have the Word of God at all. Moses and the early Israelites had only the first few books of the Bible (the Pentateuch). King David had less than half the Old Testament. Even the apostle Paul had only the Old Testament. Early Christians to the fourth century had only the relatively few copies that were made and circulated in their communities. Christians from the fourth through sixteenth centuries had to be content with those few versions that existed prior to the King James—which were usually not even produced in their own language. Christians from the seventeenth to the nineteenth centuries had only the King James Version and a few others. And, until the use of the printing press became widespread, the vast majority of believers couldn't even *own* a Bible. Copies were simply too expensive—even if they were available. Christians had to rely upon what was proclaimed at church services.

By comparison, Christians of today are immeasurably richer— not only to have the King James translation, but to also have reliable modern versions. All believers should give thanks for the great wealth they do have rather than argue over the relatively minor differences among translations.

If you are a Christian who uses the King James Version—if you understand what you read and are comfortable with it—then by all means continue to use it. If you are a Christian who uses a good modern translation, you should also feel free to continue to use it. Don't be deterred or intimidated by those who would tell you that you do not have the true Word of God in your hands.

ANSWERING BART EHRMAN:
Did the Church Scribes Change the Text of Scripture?

November 1, 2005 marked the start of a revolution in the way postmodern readers view the text of the Bible. With the release of Dr. Bart Ehrman's *Misquoting Jesus*, the everyday reader of religion has been allowed access into the often mysterious field of New Testament textual criticism, opening eyes and providing more questions than answers regarding the compilation of the sacred Christian Scriptures.

A *Publishers Weekly* review on the back cover of *Misquoting Jesus* boldly proclaims:

> Engaging and fascinating...[Ehrman's] absorbing story, fresh and lively prose, and seasoned insights into the challenges of recreating the texts of the New Testament ensure that readers might never read the Gospels or Paul's letters the same way again.

Over 250,000 copies of the hardcover edition sold in the first four months of the book's publication, with no slowdown in sight. The overwhelming amount of media attention given to the title has not escaped the notice of the conservative evangelical Christian community.

The *Dallas Morning News* interviewed Ehrman and quoted some excerpts from the interview:

"Most of the differences [in the New Testament] don't matter, but some of the differences are huge," said Bart Ehrman…the author of *Misquoting Jesus,* a book that suggests sections of the New Testament were changed over the early centuries of Christianity.

Dr. Ehrman admits, however, that no major tenet of mainstream Christianity rests solely on disputed texts. Most of the details in the disputed last verses of Mark, for example, are found elsewhere in the New Testament.

But original versions of some passages support different interpretations of the nature and mission of Jesus, he said.

"In some instances, the choice affects the meaning of an entire passage, or even an entire book," he said.

For example, in *Misquoting Jesus,* he cites Luke's account of John baptizing Jesus. Modern translations have God saying, "You are my beloved son in whom I am well pleased." But Dr. Ehrman says the original said something quite different: "You are my son. Today I have begotten you."[1]

The *Dallas Morning News* is not alone in providing newsprint for Dr. Ehrman's views regarding what could be called a "remake" of the New Testament.

Another review noted, "A prolific writer, Ehrman has become a relentless skeptic of the traditional understanding of the New Testament, its message, and its history. He has appeared on CNN, the Discovery Channel, and even Jon Stewart's *Daily Show.* And he delights in 'taking something really complicated and getting a sound bite out of it.'"[2]

Reactions have varied greatly. Many Christian leaders and lay people have labeled *Misquoting Jesus* as heresy. On the other end of the spectrum are many scholars and others who have embraced the popularity of *Misquoting Jesus,* proclaiming it an accurate portrayal of church history and the Bible's transmission. But is there a third option? While *Misquoting Jesus* may include some accurate information about portions of the New Testament's history, many aspects are skewed to make the author's point, standing on very flimsy historical evidence.

I (John) discussed some of these controversies with Dr. Daniel Wallace, professor of New Testament at Dallas Theological Seminary. In addition to discovering new manuscripts and serving as a translator for some of today's English translations, Wallace has personally debated Bart Ehrman on some of the issues of controversy presented in *Misquoting Jesus*.

Identifying the Issues

In our interview together,[3] Wallace first noted, "I have always found Bart to be a very congenial fellow, nice guy, fun to talk to. And yet he has moved very far to the left since his days at Princeton. He started out at Moody, then he went to Wheaton, got his master's degree at Princeton, and his doctorate at Princeton. And his book *Misquoting Jesus* is kind of the latest coming-out of where he is on these issues that are very dear to his heart, which is the text of the New Testament. The essential aspect of *Misquoting Jesus* is that we can't tell what the original [Scripture] text said, but what we can tell is it probably was not as fully orthodox as most of our manuscripts seem to suggest that it is."

Further issues with Ehrman's views were also mentioned by Wallace: "...they are asking questions like, 'Can we really know that we have the Bible, what was written originally or something very close to it?' 'Are doctrines being played with because of these differences?' That kind of thing.

"You know, Bart's story is not unusual. The introductory chapter to Craig Evans's book *Fabricating Jesus,* which is a terrific book, goes through the biographies of many people writing about Jesusanity and against Christianity. And almost every one of those stories belongs to someone who grew up in a home that was Bible-believing and included very conservative Christianity. What you see as he goes through these biographies is a kind of what I call brittle fundamentalism, where there is a particular view of the way the Scripture operates, and if there is one violation of it, it isn't just that your view changes, it shatters.

"So you go from one end of the spectrum and move very, very quickly to the other end of it. You feel so burned about the experience that you want to turn around and make sure no one else goes through what you went through. I think that is an element of Bart's story. I think many people who write in this area have ended up teaching in university settings. And the questions they ask are, at one level, very legitimate questions that deserve answers. They deserve to be engaged. You can't simply say, well, that's liberal or disrespectful. No, in some cases they are asking very sincere questions that deserve careful attention."

The Facts on the New Testament Manuscripts

In our conversation I asked Dr. Wallace, "Do we have manuscripts that go back very close to Jesus and the apostles?"

Wallace responded, "I think what we need to say is Bart [Ehrman] gives this image that we don't have manuscripts almost for hundreds of years at all. At one place when he was on a television or a radio show he actually said that. But he knows this is not the case. I am not so sure he can say we don't have copies of copies of copies of copies. We don't know how many generations there are between the copies we do have and the original. But this we do know: We have in the second century [A.D. 100–199] between ten to fifteen manuscript copies, all of them are fragmentary, all are papyri, but they are all from the New Testament. That is absolutely unheard of for any other Greco-Roman literature. You don't have any other ancient Greco-Roman literature that has copies that come within decades of the original documents. Yet people are saying we can't possibly know what the original New Testament said. If that is true about the New Testament, it is a hundred times more true of all the other ancient documents."

As Dr. Wallace finished his introductory remarks, he went on to say:

"The imagery that Bart [Ehrman] is trying to present with this, I think, is an imagery we are all familiar with. It is the telephone game we all played as kids. The whole point of the telephone game is to whisper something in somebody's ear, and the next nine or ten people pass along this message, and when you get to the last one, he tells a garbled message, and everybody laughs. The whole point of the game is to see how badly a message can get garbled. And so it is not necessarily a coherent message to begin with...But there are a lot of problems with using that analogy, whether Ehrman uses it explicitly or implicitly. First, we are dealing with written documents. We're not dealing with words spoken in a parlor game...so if you have a document like the Gospel of John written down, and the next guy is supposed to write it down, is he going to garble it as much as the guy who is hearing these words? That is not likely. Secondly, you have multiple lines of transmission. It is not just an original person going through a single line of people. Instead, you have three or four lines going out.

"So you have these lines of transmission from these original documents. Now, if you compare just the last person in each one of those lines with their documents and compare them to each other, we would have a far better sense of what that original document actually said. But third, you are not limited to consulting the last person. We can consult several of the intermediary agents and get back much closer to the original message. So if I say I am going to pick the number three guy in this line, and the number four guy in this line, and the number six guy in this line, out of 300 guys we can get very, very close to the original. We can make comparisons. And finally, that original document would have been copied far more than just one time.

"Again, it is not just one line of transmission, but it is several lines, maybe even ten or twenty lines through which this document is being copied. And those developed their own streams of transmission. When you see the Bible text in that light, we can say that is so different from the telephone game and so different from the impression that we are getting from reading *Misquoting Jesus*— that I think what we have here is something that tells us what the original text said."

Dealing with the Differences

Our conversation then shifted to dealing with the variations that do exist between the existing copies of the Greek New Testament. Ehrman has claimed there are as many as 400,000 textual variants. Is that correct? And if so, how can we consider the New Testament to have been accurately copied?

Wallace acknowledged, "Ehrman is absolutely right when he says there are as many as 400,000 textual variants among our manuscripts. But what he doesn't communicate very clearly is that these differences are, for the most part, absolutely irrelevant. Seventy-five percent of them are spelling differences or nonsense errors. There is one, for example, in 1 Thessalonians 2:7 where we have a famous textual problem where Paul says that we became 'gentle' among you or we became 'little children' among you. And the difference between 'gentle' and 'little children,' in the Greek text, is one letter. There is also one manuscript that has 'we became huppoi' that is, we became horses among you. Well, that's what you call a nonsense reading. Nobody is going to think that is authentic. That still counts as a textual variant, even though the guy had too much caffeine that day and didn't know what he was doing.

"The fact is, all of those variants, nonsense or not, count as textual variants. And 75 percent of them are going to be nonsense variants or simply spelling differences...The next two chunks would be almost 25 percent, and that includes word order changes, because in Greek you can change the word order without changing what the subject is. If you say 'Jesus loves John,' you can actually have the word order 'John loves Jesus,' but anybody who knows Greek knows that Jesus is the subject and John is the object because of the endings on those words.

"There are at least eighteen different ways to write 'Jesus loves John' without any spelling variations between those two at all. If you have spelling variations you have just doubled it to 36 in terms of one of the names. And then you have some other little particles and then some differences in terms of how you have the word 'love.' My estimate is you have somewhere between 500 to 1000 ways to say 'Jesus loves John' in Greek without essentially changing the meaning at all. That is the potential number of variants we have on that three-word text."

Factor this number of variations with approximately 30,000 manuscripts, and we can easily understand how there could technically be 400,000 variants, yet experts can still correctly say that the New Testament text has been accurately transmitted.

Meaningful and Viable

If 75 percent of the 400,000 variants were spelling or nonsensical errors that did not have any impact on the text when compared with other texts, and 24 percent of the remaining variants had to do with differences in word order that do not change the meaning of the text, then what about the remaining one percent of variants? It was here that Wallace explained his distinction between meaningful and viable discrepancies in the text:

"The next largest category is those textual variants that are meaningful, but they are not viable. And by viable I mean they cannot go back to the original text, because they are found in one fourteenth-century manuscript or a twelfth-century manuscript that has no history that suggests that it goes back to the original. That is a fairly large group.

"The smallest group of textual variants we have—it's less than one percent—are those variants that are both meaningful and viable. That means we are dealing with much less than one percent of all these 400,000 textual variants that are going to impact anything. And the question is, what do they impact?"

In other words, of the less than one percent of variants that remain uncertain, would any of them cause us to question our Christian doctrine in some way?

When I put this question to Dr. Wallace, he returned to the doubts presented by Dr. Bart Ehrman in *Misquoting Jesus*. "I think this is the impression Ehrman tries to give, but he doesn't produce the evidence that shows that. And so people read his book and they have this Chicken Little mentality that says, 'My gosh, the sky is falling. I don't know what to believe anymore.' But you start looking at the evidence. You say, the deity of Christ is untouched by these viable variants, the virgin birth is untouched, the resurrection of Christ is untouched. Everything that the Bible teaches that is a cardinal truth, an essential truth, is found there in the manuscripts and is untouched by the variants."

Evaluating Specifics

As we moved beyond general principles to specific verses, I pressed Wallace on some of the individual verses argued in *Misquoting Jesus* as being inauthentic.

Mark 16:9-20—The Longer Ending of Mark

One passage Bart Ehrman uses to question the reliability of the New Testament is the final 12 verses of the Gospel of Mark. As a kind of shock tactic, he says, in effect, "Look, do you realize you ought to knock off the last twelve verses of the Gospel of Mark?" As if that were to call into question the rest of the New Testament. I asked Dr. Wallace his thoughts.

He said, "It has been known for at least 125 years that those last twelve verses are probably not authentic. And there's no doctrinal statement for any evangelical school or church that I know of that includes these twelve verses. Mark 16:9-20 must be in our Bible; it's an important story. But the fact is, whether that's part of Scripture or not does not impact any fundamental doctrine."

In fact, if you look at Mark 16:9-20 in modern Bible translations, you will see a footnote that states these verses are disputed and not part of the earliest manuscripts.

John 7:53–8:11–The Woman Caught in Adultery

Another example is the story of the woman taken in adultery. This is said to be an addition to the New Testament.

Wallace answered, "I agree with [Erhman] that John 7:53–8:11 is not part of what John wrote. And here's the question I like to ask people. I say, 'This is my favorite passage that's not in the Bible.' Then I ask, 'If you had to make a choice between Mark 16:9-20 and John 7:53–8:11, and you could have only one of those passages in the Bible, which would you choose? So far, every place I've gone asked that question, people have said they would pick John 7:53–8:11. And it's a passage that the ancient scribes wanted as well. It has less testimony for it than Mark 16 does, the longer passage. So on the basis of text critical principles, we have to agree with Ehrman, this passage is out."

1 John 5:7–The Case for the Trinity

First John 5:7, which explicitly defines the Trinity, is also said to be a later addition to the New Testament. I asked Dr. Wallace bluntly, "Give us the verse and tell us—should it be in, or should it be out?"

Wallace responded, "In the King James Bible, 1 John 5:7 says, 'There are three that bear record in heaven, the Father, the Word, and the Holy Ghost, and these three are one.' This verse was added to the Bible in 1522 when Erasmus, who was the first publisher of any Greek New Testament, was pressured from the church to add this Trinitarian statement because it had been found in some Latin manuscripts. There was some scribe by the name of Roy working in 1520 at Oxford, and he writes out this Greek New Testament, and it somehow gets into Eramus's hands. And Erasmus never made the promise that he'd put it in if he found such a manuscript, but he basically said the reverse: 'I didn't put it in because I didn't find any manuscript.' So he finds this manuscript—I'm sure somebody brought it to his door—and he writes the words in his Greek text, and he actually changes the text from what Roy had written, because Roy didn't know Greek very well...and Erasmus had to make the fixes.

"But the verse is not found in our ancient manuscripts. It's found in four sixteenth-century manuscripts. And four manuscripts in the twelfth century or later in the marginal note, with a sixteenth- or seventeenth-century hand. That's a passage I'd have to say is not authentic, and the ancient church never even thought about it being authentic.

"Ehrman talks about this passage as if there's no way we could have ever come up with the doctrine of the Trinity without this, and therefore the Trinity is not true. But he knows what the church councils believed. He knows about the Council of Constantinople in 381 and the Council of Nicea and all the rest of these, the Chalcedonian Creed in 451, that clearly affirmed the Trinity without having this verse even in existence."

While the history of 1 John 5:7 definitely fuels Ehrman's viewpoint, it simply highlights a historical problem translators have long since corrected. To suggest that this error disproves the Trinity or the original manuscript's inerrancy is a logical fallacy. A dispute with one point of the New Testament's text does not necessarily mean the entire New Testament is flawed.

How to Respond to Ehrman and Others Like Him

So how should we respond to the writings of Ehrman and others like him?

Wallace provided the following helpful thought: "I encourage them to read Ehrman's book. He's asking the right questions. But I encourage them to not read just his book. They should read our book as well, *Dethroning Jesus,* and others like it…They should ask these questions, but they should not start with a brittle fundamentalism. What they need to do is to say, 'Let me wrestle with these issues and realize that the person of Christ is more important than what I think about the Bible.' And if they understand that, then they come to the place where they revere him. And then, it's because of his [Jesus'] attitude about the Bible that they can have, I think, the right attitude about Scripture as well."

PART THREE:

What Is *in* the Bible?

11

THE CULTURE OF THE BIBLE:
What Does Archaeology Show Us about the Bible?

I n what ways does archaeology[1] help us view the Bible as accurate? One is that archaeology can help affirm some of the biblical accounts of events, places, or people. Obviously we cannot expect archaeology to confirm *every* statement of biblical history, geography, or culture because the amount of information archaeology has uncovered is still small. But that which *has* been uncovered has confirmed the biblical record repeatedly.

The New International Dictionary of Biblical Archaeology, written by a team of experts in various fields, repeatedly vindicates the biblical account of history. To illustrate, the editor's preface remarks,

> Near Eastern archaeology has demonstrated the historical and geographical reliability of the Bible in many important areas. By clarifying the objectivity and factual accuracy of biblical authors, archaeology also helps correct the view that the Bible is avowedly partisan and subjective. It is now known, for instance, that, along with the Hittites, Hebrew scribes were the best historians in the entire ancient Near East, despite contrary propaganda that emerged from Assyria, Egypt, and elsewhere.[2]

John Arthur Thompson formerly served as the director of the Australian Institute of Archaeology in Melbourne. In *The Bible and Archaeology* he writes,

Finally, it is perfectly true to say that biblical archaeology has done a great deal to correct the impression that was abroad at the close of the last century and in the early part of this century, that biblical history was of doubtful trustworthiness in many places. If one impression stands out more clearly than any other today, it is that on all hands the overall historicity of the Old Testament tradition is admitted. In this connection the words of W.F. Albright may be quoted: "There can be no doubt that archaeology has confirmed the substantial historicity of Old Testament traditions."[3]

Norman Geisler and Ron Brooks point out, "In every period of Old Testament history, we find that there is good evidence from archaeology that the scriptures are accurate...While many have doubted the accuracy of the Bible, time and continued research have consistently demonstrated that the Word of God is better informed than its critics."[4]

For example, many aspects of Bible books have been confirmed against the views of critics—in particular, the books written by Moses and the books of Daniel, Ezra, Kings, and Acts. Daniel, for example, because of its supernatural predictions, was dated by critics to the time of the Maccabees, around 165 B.C., rather than in the sixth century B.C. during the lifetime of Daniel. Critics had also doubted the exile and the return of the Jews as mentioned in the book of Esther, as well as the official government decrees involving the exile and return. Further, critics said the chronological records of the books of Kings were hopelessly confused.

Now, however, archaeologist Dr. Clifford Wilson and others have provided many examples of how archaeology has confirmed the accuracy of these books. In his *Rocks, Relics and Biblical Reliability*, Dr. Wilson supplies examples, some of which we quote below:

> There are other evidences of eyewitness recording by Daniel. That he knew Nebuchadnezzar rebuilt Babylon (Dan. 4:30)

is a problem by those who argue for a later date for Daniel. This fact of history was recovered by excavation only in modern times, yet Daniel had recorded it correctly. One critic wrote that this was a difficulty, the answer to which "we shall presumably never know"...Linguistic pointers from the Dead Sea Scrolls (e.g., a recent targum of Job) also suggest an early, not a late, date for Daniel...The overthrow of the non-historical view of the Exile and the return of the Jews came with the finding of the famous Cyrus Cylinder...By this decree [of King Cyrus] the Hebrew people were given leave to rebuild the temple in Jerusalem...The same can be said about the style of writing in the Book of Ezra, for as Albright says, "If we turn to the Book of Ezra, recent discoveries have indicated the authenticity of its official documents in the most striking way." Albright shows that the language of Ezra had been seriously challenged, but that some of the very words that have been challenged have turned up in Egyptian, Aramaic, and Babylonian cuneiform documents that date to the exact time of Ezra. Albright goes on: "If it were practicable to quote from still unpublished Aramaic documents from fifth century Egypt, the weight of factual evidence would crush all opposition"...Still another convincing evidence of the genuineness of the Bible records is in *The Mysterious Numbers of the Hebrew Kings* by Edwin R. Thiele. Where once it seemed that the dates of the kings in the divided-kingdom period were inaccurate and vague, he has been able to show remarkable synchronisms...Once again, an area that many believed was total confusion has been shown to be staggeringly accurate recording, with fine chronological interweaving that cannot be claimed for any other book of ancient history.[5]

The reliability of the New Testament is also confirmed by archaeological data. In the case of the book of Acts,

it is widely agreed today that in this book [Acts] we can see the hand of a historian of the first rank...Luke is shown to be a most careful recorder of information, whether it be matters of geography and political boundaries, local customs, titles of local officers, local religious practices, details of local topography, or the disposition of buildings in Greek or Roman, Asian or European towns.[6]

A.N. Sherwin-White remarks, "For Acts the confirmation of historicity is overwhelming...Any attempt to reject its basic historicity must now appear absurd. Roman historians have long taken it for granted."[7]

Consider some examples of Luke's accuracy in historical reporting:

Luke demonstrated a remarkably accurate knowledge of geographical and political ideas. He referred correctly to provinces that were established at that time, as indicated in Acts 15:41; 16:2, 6-8. He identified regions, such as that referred to in Acts 13:49, and various cities, as in Acts 14:6. He demonstrated a clear knowledge of local customs, such as those relating to the speech of the Lycaonians (Acts 14:11), some aspects relating to the foreign woman who was converted at Athens (Acts 17:34), and he even knew that the city of Ephesus was known as "the temple-keeper of Artemis" (Acts 19:35)...he refers to different local officers by their exact titles—the proconsul (deputy) of Cyprus (Acts 13:7), the magistrates at Philippi (Acts 16:20, 35), the politarchs (another word for magistrates) at Thessalonica (Acts 17:6), the proconsul of Achaia (Acts 18:12), and the treasurer of Corinth (Aedile)—which was the title of the man known as Erastus at Corinth (Acts 19:22; Rom. 16:23)...

Luke had accurate knowledge about various local events such as the famine in the days of Claudius Caesar (Acts 11:29); he was aware that Zeus and Hermes were worshiped together at Lystra, though this was unknown to modern historians (Acts 14:11, 12). He knew that Diana or Artemis

was especially the goddess of the Ephesians (Acts 19:28);
and he was able to describe the trade at Ephesus in religious
images (Acts 19:26-27).[8]

As Merrill C. Tenney, professor of New Testament, points out of
Luke's writings, the Gospel of Luke and the book of Acts, "The two
volumes he wrote comprise at least one-fourth of the total canon
of the New Testament and provide the only piece of continuous
historical writing that covers the period from the birth of Jesus
of Nazareth to the establishment of a church in the capitol of the
Roman Empire."[9]

In other words, the fact that Luke has been established as such
a careful writer means that fully one-fourth of the entire New Testament, on the basis of his accuracy alone, bears the same marks
of authenticity.

It was also this same careful historian, the physician Luke, who
reported that Jesus Christ was resurrected from the dead "by many
convincing proofs"—and that he had carefully investigated the evidence for this from the beginning (Luke 1:1-4; Acts 1:1-3). If Luke
provided such great accuracy in his *historical* reporting, on what
logical basis can we assume he was inaccurate in his reporting of
matters of greater importance not only to him but to others?

Noted biblical scholar and apologist Dr. John Warwick Montgomery summarizes the evidence when he writes, "Modern
archaeological research has confirmed again and again the reliability
of New Testament geography, chronology, and general history."[10] Dr.
Wilson concludes in agreement, "Those who know the facts now
recognize that the New Testament must be accepted as a remarkably accurate source book…"[11]

In general, the entire Bible has been strikingly confirmed. Given
the large amount of data uncovered over the last 200 years, this is
no insignificant conclusion. There are literally thousands of opportunities for archaeological research to indisputably prove the Bible
false—yet it has never done so.

Silencing Skeptics

Perhaps more significant is the fact liberal theologians and secular academics cannot deny that archaeology has confirmed the biblical record at many points. Three of the greatest American archaeologists of the twentieth century each had their perspectives modified by their archaeological work. W.F. Albright, Nelson Glueck, and George Ernest Wright all received training in the liberal scholarship of the day, predominantly that of German scholars. This liberal training promoted a low view of the Bible, but as these men conducted archaeological research, their confidence in the biblical text increased significantly.

Albright admitted that he attempted to be rational and empirical in his approach to the Bible, yet he read into it with his own bias. Albright, the son of a Methodist missionary, came to see that much of German critical thought was established upon a philosophical base that could not be sustained in the light of archaeological discoveries. Nelson Glueck was Albright's student. In his own explorations in Trans-Jordan and Negev and in his excavations, Glueck worked with the Bible in hand. He trusted what he called "the remarkable phenomenon of historical memory in the Bible." He was the president of the prestigious Hebrew Union College-Jewish Institute of Religion and an ordained rabbi. And Wright went from the faculty of the McCormick Theological Seminary in Chicago to a position in the Harvard Divinity School, which he retained until his death. He, too, was a student of Albright.

Glueck stated in no uncertain terms, "It may be clearly stated categorically that no archaeological discovery has ever controverted a single biblical reference. Scores of archaeological findings have been made which confirm in clear outline or exact detail historical statements in the Bible."[12]

And, in fact, this is true not just for the patriarchal tradition but the Bible as a whole. Archaeology has repeatedly shown itself accurate rather than distorted on issues and details of history.

Consider just a few examples of hundreds that could be cited. In all the following examples, and many more, critics originally doubted what the Bible declared. Allegedly, the Bible was inaccurate in regard to these places, people, and physical items. Thus, critics concluded that the Bible was merely a human document and not very trustworthy. But thanks to archaeology, it was the authority of the critics that was silenced, not the authority of the Bible. Archaeology has confirmed the historicity and biblical time frame of...

1. Abraham and the patriarchs and the city of Ur (Genesis 11:28-31).

2. Moses as author of Genesis through Leviticus.

3. The five cities of the plain (Genesis 14:2).

4. Numerous biblical cities.

5. The use of straw in making bricks (Exodus 15:13-18).

6. The approximate date and route of the exodus.

7. Sennacherib's failure to capture Jerusalem and his death at the hands of his own sons (2 Kings 19:35-37).

8. Jehoiachin's exile in Babylon (2 Kings 25:27-30).

9. The unconquered status of the cities of Lachish and Azekah (Jeremiah 34:7).

10. Ezekiel's dating of events by the years "of the exile of king Jehoiachin" (Ezekiel 1:1).

11. The psalms of David as a tenth-century composition and the book of Daniel as a sixth-century B.C. composition (every chapter in Daniel but one clearly states this).

12. Nabonidus and Belshazzar (Daniel 5).

13. The time of Nehemiah's return and Sanballat and Tobiah as his enemies (Nehemiah 2:1,10,19; 4:1-3,7-8; 6:1ff).

14. The drachma coin in Nehemiah (Nehemiah 7:70).

15. The census at the time of Christ's birth (Luke 2:1-3).

16. Sergius Paulus, the proconsul of Paphos (Acts 13:6-7).

17. The relationship between Iconium, Lystra, and Derbe (Acts 14:6).

18. The district of Macedonia (Acts 16:12).

19. The magistrates of Philippi (Acts 16:20).

20. Herod's temple and winter palace (Matthew 2:4; Luke 1:9).

21. The pools of Siloam and Bethesda (John 5:2; 9:7).

22. Peter's house (Matthew 8:14).

23. Jacob's well (John 4:5-6).

24. Artemis's temple, statues, and altar (Acts 19:27-28,35).

25. The Ephesian theatre and Golden House of Nero (Acts 19:29; 25:10; 1 Peter 2:13).

These examples illustrate the Bible's historical reliability. By 1958, "over 25,000 sites from the biblical world have been confirmed by some archaeological discoveries to date."[13]

According to the Experts

In an interview with respected Jewish archaeologist Dr. Gabriel Barkay, who has been awarded the top prize for archaeological research in Israel, I (John) asked him if he thought that the writers of the New Testament anchored their stories in real historical events. Based on his research, he confidently replied, "Yes, I do. I think that much of the evidence of the Gospels mirrors a reality of the first century."[14]

In fact, in a prime-time television program I (John) filmed on location in Israel, Christian and non-Christian scholars alike repeatedly confirmed the integrity of the New Testament's historical accounts. Dr. Magen Broshi, former curator of the Shrine of the Book, Israel's museum of the Dead Sea Scrolls, said this about the historical record found in the New Testament: "The setting is absolutely accurate. The geography is accurate. The mode of living...they couldn't have invented it, and they didn't have any need to invent anything."

Respected Jewish archaeologist Dr. Hillel Geva concurred with Broshi's words. Having worked on some of the most important archaeological excavations in Jerusalem since 1967, he is editor of the leading Hebrew journal on biblical archaeology in Israel. He notes that "the New Testament is a very authentic, historical book. No doubt there is history in it—real and authentic history in the book." In total, archaeologists have confirmed that Luke cited facts about 32 countries, 54 cities, 9 islands, and several rulers, and he never made a single mistake.

Let's look now at a few of the archaeological finds that support the accuracy of the biblical accounts of the life of Jesus.

Jesus' Birthplace

Bethlehem, Israel is the traditional birthplace of Jesus and therefore a holy site of Christians around the world. In 2001, I (John) traveled with a team to record a television series on location there. The area is now a bustling city.

The very location of Jesus' birth is where the mother of the Roman emperor Constantine built the Church of the Nativity in the fourth century A.D. The site has been revered by Christians since Justin Martyr identified it in the mid-second century.

Apparently the account of Jesus' birth in Bethlehem was so well known in the early second century that not only was the Roman emperor aware of the birthplace, but he was also aware of the specific location of the cave within Bethlehem. Early in the second century, as a deliberate insult to Christianity, the emperor Hadrian planted a grove of trees in honor of the god Adonis at the place where Jesus was born:

> Both Jerome and Paulinus of Nola provide evidence that the cave in Bethlehem, under the present Church of the Nativity, was identified as the birthplace [of Jesus] before the time of [the Roman emperor] Hadrian—thus almost into the first century. Hadrian (117–38) marked the site by

planting a grove of trees there in honor of the Roman god
Adonis.[15]

Clearly, the knowledge of Jesus' birth as recorded in Matthew and
Luke was widespread in the early to mid-second century. What's the
best explanation for how that came to be the case? There's little to
support the theory that Christians were making up stories and were
speaking only for highly isolated communities within the Christian
world. It makes the most sense that Matthew and Luke recorded
information that was considered credible by the earliest Christians
around the world, including Jesus' relatives.[16]

Dr. Darrell Bock, research professor of New Testament at Dallas
Theological Seminary, says, "I think He was born in Bethlehem. In
fact, again, let's take the alternative. What evidence is there that He
was born in Nazareth? And my response would be, 'Silence.' There
is none."[17] Dr. D.S. Pfann, a professor living in Israel, also made
the very important point that there is no other account of the place
where Jesus was born: "There's only one tradition concerning Jesus'
birthplace, and that's Bethlehem."[18]

Dr. Pfann, the director of the Jerusalem School for the Study of
Early Christianity and of the Nazareth Village noted in an interview,
"The tradition of a birth site like Bethlehem is actually strengthened
by the fact that the earliest record that we have of the tradition of
Jesus' birthplace goes back to Justin Martyr, who 15-20 years after
Bethlehem was totally destroyed by Roman armies, said that the
pilgrims came to visit a cave. We go there today. It's at the top of
a hill, which is just where a patriarchal home would be built—on
top of a hill. Patriarchal homes are kept for many generations, and
kept within the family. So the tradition of Jesus' birthplace there
in the middle of the second century is actually extremely close to
the time when those homes were still in existence in Bethlehem.
So knowing that Jesus was born there, that his family's patriarchal
home would have persisted there until their destruction around
A.D. 137, and then just 15 or 20 years later Justin Martyr states that's

where people commemorated his birth, actually brings it into the category of probably being the place where Jesus was born."[19]

The City of Nazareth

The name of the city of Nazareth is not mentioned in the Old Testament or any other ancient Jewish sources. However, in 1961, an early Hebrew inscription was found in Caesarea that mentions Nazareth. During Jesus' time, Nazareth would have had a population of about 500. This matches the New Testament picture that portrayed Nazareth as an obscure, unnoteworthy village. In the Gospel of John, people who hear of Jesus of Nazareth ask themselves, "What good could come from Nazareth?"[20]

In the Gospel accounts, we find that Nazareth was the home of Jesus' mother Mary and of Joseph.[21] It was the site of the angelic announcement to Mary that she would give birth to the Savior, and it was the town where Jesus grew up.[22]

According to respected Jewish archaeologist Dr. Magen Broshi, in an on-location interview regarding the early life of Jesus, the [details] about Jesus' hometown in the New Testament "fits very well of what we know about first century Palestine. They fit very well because they give us a good picture of what was happening here, and archaeology can prove it."[23]

Jacob's Well

In John 4, we read about Jesus carrying on a conversation with a Samaritan woman at a place called Jacob's Well. The site still exists, though the well is now usually quite dry and dysfunctional. It is at the entrance to the valley between Ebal and Gerizim, about two miles southeast of Shechem. It is about nine feet in diameter and about 75 feet deep, though in ancient times it was no doubt much deeper—probably twice as deep. The digging of such a well must have been a very time-intensive and costly undertaking.

One expert states:

Unfortunately, the well of Jacob has not escaped that misplaced religious worship of holy sites. A series of buildings of various styles, and of different ages, have cumbered the ground, choked up the well, and disfigured the natural beauty and simplicity of the spot. At present the rubbish in the well has been cleared out, but there is still a domed structure over it, and you gaze down the shaft cut in the living rock and see at a depth of 70 feet the surface of the water glimmering with a pale blue light in the darkness, while you notice how the limestone blocks that form its curb have been worn smooth, or else furrowed by the ropes of centuries.[24]

As Jesus conversed with the Samaritan woman at this well, she spoke of physical water, and Jesus changed the subject to spiritual water, or the water of life (Jesus himself). He noted her marital background as if all-knowing and convinced her he was a prophet. By the end of their discussion, the woman abandoned her water jug, headed back to the village, and asked people, "Come, see a man who told me everything I ever did. Could this be the Christ?"[25]

Jesus stayed two more days in the area, and many of the villagers came to believe in him as the Messiah. For a Samaritan village, a group culturally hostile with Jews, such a change would have indicated a monumental transformation. For John's original audience, this would have been considered nothing less than a miracle. Samaritans believing in a carpenter Jew as the coming Messiah? According to John, this was clear evidence that Jesus was God's Son.

The Synagogue in Capernaum

The Jewish synagogue in Capernaum lies on the shore of the Sea of Galilee in Israel. It was in this town where Jesus taught "as one who had authority, and not as the teachers of the law" (Mark 1:22). The synagogue is where Jesus was confronted by a demon-possessed man while teaching (Mark 1:21-27), where he healed the servant of the centurion (Luke 7:3), and where he gave his message on the bread of life (John 6:35-59).[26] If this synagogue could be found, it would offer another cultural insight regarding the life of Jesus and the reliability of his friends' statements about him.

Fortunately, this synagogue has been rediscovered. One excavation's feedback notes that "among today's remains of Capernaum lies a fourth-century synagogue of white limestone. The foundation of this synagogue is constructed of black basaltic stone, probably dating to the first-century synagogue built by the Roman centurion who was stationed in Capernaum in Luke 7:5."[27] In other words, the synagogue has been accurately noted as existing during the lifetime of Jesus. Jesus' teachings match the terrain because Capernaum thrived as a fishing village, and researchers today have noted many other connections with additional Gospel parallels. While this does not prove that Jesus is God's Son or that he healed anyone, it does show that what Jesus' friends said about him fits within what is known by archaeologists of his contemporary surroundings and culture.

The Tomb of Lazarus

One of the most remarkable miracles communicated from the lifetime of Jesus is the revival of Lazarus four days after his death. In contrast with what modern skeptics say, multiple ancient Christian writings indicate that the tomb from which Lazarus rose from the dead was visited by later generations. For instance:

- The early church historian Eusebius, writing around A.D. 330, noted that the place of Lazarus is still known.

- In A.D. 333, a guide pointed out to the Pilgrim of Bordeaux the "crypt" where Lazarus had been laid to rest.

- In A.D. 390, St. Jerome makes mention of a church built near the "place of Lazarus."

The first catacomb found near Bethany was investigated by renowned French archaeologist Charles Clermont-Ganneau. The other, a large burial cemetery unearthed near the modern Dominus Flevit Chapel, was excavated by Italian scholar P. Bagatti.

Both archaeologists found evidence clearly dating the two catacombs to the first century A.D., with the latter finding coins minted by Governor Varius Gratus at the turn of the millenium (up to A.D. 15/16). Evidence in both catacombs indicated their use for burial until the middle part of the first century A.D., several years before the New Testament was written.

The first catacomb was a family tomb investigated by archaeologist Clermont-Ganneau on the Mount of Olives near the ancient town of Bethany. There, he was surprised to find names that corresponded with names that appear in the New Testament. Even more interesting were the signs of the cross etched on several of the ossuaries (stone coffins).

As Clermont-Ganneau further investigated the tomb, he found inscriptions, including the names of Eleazar (Lazarus), Martha, and Mary on three different coffins.[28]

Again, such archaeological finds do not prove that Jesus raised Lazarus from the dead. But they do indicate that Jesus was a literal person who visited a particular area at the time his friends said he lived. Unlike many religions, in which the leaders are entirely mythical or nonphysical in nature, Jesus is known as a religious leader who lived and taught among the common people of his day. For those who examine the information, the historical evidence from Christian, Jewish, and Greco-Roman sources all record that Jesus healed the sick, sent away demons, and even raised Lazarus from the dead.

Pilate's Stone

It wasn't long ago when many scholars were questioning the actual existence of a Roman governor with the name Pontius Pilate, the procurator who ordered Jesus' crucifixion. In June 1961, Italian archaeologists led by Dr. Frova were excavating an ancient Roman amphitheatre near Caesarea-on-the-Sea and uncovered an interesting limestone block. On the face is a monumental inscription which is part of a larger dedication to Tiberius Caesar, which clearly says that it was from "Pontius Pilate, Prefect of Judea."[29]

The inscription reads as follows:

TIBERIEUM,

[PON]*TIUS*

[PRAEF]*ECTUS IUDA*[EAE]

The only written information regarding Pontius Pilate outside of the New Testament comes from two Jewish writers: Josephus, and Philo of Alexandria. Both writers noted that at one time Pilate had placed golden shields on the walls of his palace on Mt. Zion. These shields had inscriptions that mentioned the names of various gods. Tiberius personally ordered the removal of the shields. Another time Pilate used temple revenues to build his aqueduct (water lines). There is another incident recorded only in the Bible (Luke 13:1), where Pilate ordered the slaughter of certain Galileans who had supposedly been offering sacrifices in the Temple.[30]

When the 2004 Mel Gibson film *The Passion of the Christ* hit theaters, our friend Dr. Darrell Bock was interviewed on ABC with Diane Sawyer regarding his thoughts on the movie's accuracy. Shortly afterward, I (John) interviewed Darrell for *The John Ankerberg Show,* and asked for his extended thoughts on the film's portrayal of Pilate and the death of Jesus.

His words match what we see in this archaeological find concerning Pilate: "I think this is the most accurate film that we've had yet of Jesus' final hours. It doesn't step back from the violence of crucifixion…It also gets into the tensions of first-century politics in an effective way—particularly the complexity of Jesus' relationship to the Jewish leadership as well as the complexity of the Jewish relationship to Pilate and to Rome. And it does so in a way that shows the tensions of first-century politics and the inconsistencies in some of the relationships as they waffle and waver to figure out exactly how to deal with what they perceive to be a difficult situation."[31]

Archaeology's Support of the Bible

When asked about the importance of archaeology in the life of Jesus, Dr. Craig Evans, a New Testament professor who has lectured at Cambridge, Durham, Oxford, and at conferences around the world, shared in an interview that "archaeology doesn't prove that Jesus was really God's Son. But what it does is that it shows that there is a historical foundation on which confessions of faith make perfectly good sense."[32]

Archaeology helps us better understand what Jesus' friends wrote about him in the Bible. If the historical, geographical, and cultural details they recorded are reliable, then what remains is to make a decision as to whether the details about his supernatural acts, such as his claim to be God and his resurrection, are real parts of history. If so, then we are faced with someone who urged us to change our lives to follow and serve him. Jesus gave an invitation to a hope-filled afterlife along with supernatural forgiveness and strength for our lives today.

Does that sound good to you? Are you at the point you realize the need to accept as true what the Bible says about the Jesus of history? Ask him to forgive your sins, enter your life, and empower you to live for him. He will do it right now if you are willing to ask him.

Given the thousands of minute details recorded in the Bible, if the Bible were only the writings of humans, archaeology would have revealed such by now. What's more, archaeology has yet to correct the Bible beyond legitimate adjustments because of new knowledge in relation to Bible backgrounds and matters such as the correct use of the titles of Israel's neighbors. Given the evidence for the historical reliability of the Bible, we now move to the issue of the miracles recorded in the Bible. Did they really happen? What can we know?

12

THE MIRACLES OF THE BIBLE:
Did Supernatural Events Really Happen?

The Bible is filled with accounts of miracles. From the Creation to the second coming, from Moses at the burning bush to Daniel in the lions' den, from the virgin birth to the resurrection, miraculous happenings fill the pages of Scripture. To the believer, these are a wonderful confirmation of the power and message of God, but to the unbeliever, miracles are a stumbling block—an alleged proof that religion is just a bunch of fairy tales. In the world of the skeptic, there is no divine intervention, no interruptions to the normal order of things. Instead, there is only what is seen. Fire consumes when it burns; lions eat whatever is available; and the dead stay dead. As far as skeptics are concerned, the miracles of the Bible could no more be true than what we read in Mother Goose.

The purpose of this chapter is not to explain how the miracles of the Bible occurred. Neither will we attempt to convince anyone that miracles should be considered part of the normal operations of the universe. Our objective is to convince people that the naturalistic attitude toward miracles that has been fostered for over the past 200 years goes against simple common sense. This naturalistic attitude is based on faulty logic and unsound thinking that has decided what it is going to find long before it finds anything.

Before we begin, we need a definition of *miracle*. One naturalistic thinker said, "The first step in this, as in all other discussions, is to come to a clear understanding as to the meaning of the term *miracles* when it is employed. Argumentation about whether miracles are possible and, if possible, credible, is mere beating the air until the arguers have agreed what they mean by the word 'miracle.'"[1] A *miracle* is divine intervention into, or interruption of, the regular course of the world that produces a purposeful but unusual event that would not have occurred otherwise. By this definition, then, natural laws are understood to be the normal, regular way the world operates. And a miracle occurs as an unusual, irregular, and specific act of a God who is beyond the universe. This does not mean that miracles are violations of natural law or even opposed to them. Miracles don't violate the regular laws of cause and effect; they simply have a cause that transcends nature.

Some Well-Known Miracles of Jesus[2]

Miracle	Scripture Passage
Turns water into wine	John 2:1-11
Orders the wind and waves to be quiet	Mark 4:35-41
Walks on water	Matthew 14:22-33
With five loaves and two fish, feeds a crowd of about 5000 people	Matthew 14:13-21
Raises Lazarus to life	John 11:17-44
Raises a dead girl to life	Matthew 9:18-26
Gives sight to a man born blind	John 9:1-41
Cures the woman who had been bleeding for 12 years	Matthew 9:20-22
Cures a man of evil spirits	Mark 5:1-20
Heals ten men with leprosy	Luke 17:11-19
Heals a crippled man	Mark 2:1-12
Heals a man who was deaf and could hardly talk	Mark 7:31-37
Heals the high priest's servant after the man's ear is cut off	Luke 22:49-52

Are Miracles Possible?

The most basic question to ask about miracles is, Are miracles possible? If they are *not* possible, we can wrap up our discussion early and go home. If they *are* possible, then we need to address the argument that claims they are absurd. We find the root of this argument in the writings of Benedict de Spinoza. He developed the following argument against miracles:

1. Miracles violate the laws of nature.
2. Natural laws are immutable.
3. It is impossible for immutable laws to be violated.
4. Therefore, miracles are not possible.

Spinoza was bold in his assertion that "nothing then, comes to pass in nature in contravention to her universal laws, nay, nothing does not agree with them and follow from them, for...she keeps a fixed and immutable order."[3]

Certainly we can't argue with the third step in that argument, for what is immutable can't be set aside. But are natural laws immutable? Is this the only definition of a miracle? Spinoza built into his premises his own view that nothing exists beyond the universe. In advance, he defined natural law as "fixed and immutable," making it impossible for miracles to occur. But today scientists understand that natural laws don't tell us what *must* happen, but only describe what usually *does* happen. They are statistical probabilities, not unchangeable facts. So we can't rule out, by definition, the possibility of miracles.

The definition Spinoza provides also carries his antisupernatural bias. It assumes that there is nothing *beyond* nature that could act *in* nature. But if God exists, then miracles are possible. If there is anything beyond the universe that might cause something to happen in the universe, then there is a chance that it will do so. Once we have established that a theistic God exists, miracles cannot be ruled out.

The basis for believing in the miraculous goes back to the biblical concept of God. Genesis 1:1 notes the first recorded miracle in the Bible, the creation of the universe. If this verse can be accepted at face value, then accepting the rest of the miracles in the Bible should be possible as well. If God has the ability to create the heavens and the earth, then a virgin birth, walking on water, feeding 5000 people with a few loaves and fish, and other miracles should not only be possible, but expected. For those who believe in the existence of God, the miraculous is at least possible.

Are Miracles Credible?

Some people don't deny the possibility of miracles. They just can't see any reason for believing they occurred. The great English skeptic David Hume advanced this famous argument against believing in miracles:

1. A miracle is a violation of the laws of nature.
2. Firm and unalterable experience has established these laws.
3. A wise man proportions his belief to the evidence.
4. Therefore, a uniform experience amounts to a proof; there is here a direct and full proof, from the nature of the fact, against the existence of any miracle.

Some see this argument as saying that miracles can't occur, but that can easily be refuted by showing that Hume is begging the question when he defines miracles as impossible. It seems that his real point is that no one should believe in miracles because experience suggests that they don't happen. For example, we have never gone to a funeral expecting the dead person to come back to life during the memorial service. Why? Because that is all we have ever experienced—dead people stay dead. But the proper way of determining whether something might have happened is not on the basis of whether we can explain it. The first question to ask is not *can* it happen, but rather, *did* it happen?

If an event can be determined as having happened but defies explanation, we still have to admit it happened, whether we can explain it or not. Consider what happened to Jesus' disciples. They experienced the miracles of Jesus, including his resurrection. They did not have explanations for these events, yet they witnessed that they had happened. So the disciples proclaimed them and no one denied them. Neither did the enemies of Jesus. They just argued that Jesus performed his miracles by the power of Satan. But the disciples didn't argue about *how* Jesus did them. They simply recorded what they had seen and heard.

As C.S. Lewis has said, if firm and unalterable experience shows that miracles really don't happen, then they don't happen. But the only way to know that is to check the evidence that indicates they *may* have occurred. That is why the evidence for Jesus' resurrection is so important.

Interestingly, two key passages of Scripture mention the eyewitness accounts used to verify the miracles of the New Testament:

> That which was from the beginning, which we have heard, which we have seen with our eyes, which we have looked at and our hands have touched—this we proclaim concerning the Word of life. The life appeared; we have seen it and testify to it, and we proclaim to you the eternal life, which was with the Father and has appeared to us. We proclaim to you what we have seen and heard, so that you also may have fellowship with us. And our fellowship is with the Father and with his Son, Jesus Christ (1 John 1:1-3).

> Many have undertaken to draw up an account of the things that have been fulfilled among us, just as they were handed down to us by those who from the first were eyewitnesses and servants of the word. Therefore, since I myself have carefully investigated everything from the beginning, it seemed good also to me to write an orderly account for you, most excellent Theophilus, so that you may know the certainty of the things you have been taught (Luke 1:1-4).

The New Testament writers noted that the miracles of Jesus were verified by many witnesses. As a result, they are based on historical reality, despite the fact that the events seem contrary to the laws of nature.

In an interview on *The John Ankerberg Show,* Oxford scholar Dr. N.T. Wright stated, "It's one of the remarkable games of contemporary history on Jesus, that a majority of current Jesus scholars, including many who are not Christian believers, agree that Jesus *did* do remarkable healings. That is the main explanation for why he attracted crowds and drew so many followers. It wasn't just that his teaching was exciting, though it was. People came because things were happening. A great aunt who had been sick for 50 years: 'Bring her and Jesus will heal her.' That draws the crowds and would do so today if it happened."[4]

Yet there are those who continue to dispute that Jesus performed miracles. Why? Dr. William Lane Craig, research professor of philosophy at Talbot School of Theology in California, suggested in our discussion that "members of the Jesus Seminar who are skeptical in their approach to the New Testament have made many of their presuppositions abundantly clear...Their number one pillar of scholarly investigation of the historical Jesus is the presupposition [or starting assumption] of naturalism—that miracles do not happen."

Of the various words used in the New Testament to speak of miracles, one of the most common is the word "sign." John notes at the end of his Gospel that "Jesus did many other miraculous signs in the presence of his disciples, which are not recorded in this book. But these are written that you may believe that Jesus is the Christ, the Son of God, and that by believing you may have life in his name" (John 20:30). The "signs" or miracles recorded in the Gospels had a specific purpose. They were not attempts by Jesus to show off.

For example, in Luke 9:12-17 we read:

> Late in the afternoon the Twelve came to him and said, "Send the crowd away so they can go to the surrounding villages and countryside and find food and lodging, because we are in a remote place here."

[Jesus] replied, "You give them something to eat."

They answered, "We have only five loaves of bread and two fish—unless we go and buy food for all this crowd." (About five thousand men were there.)

But he said to his disciples, "Have them sit down in groups of about fifty each." The disciples did so, and everybody sat down. Taking the five loaves and the two fish and looking up to heaven, he gave thanks and broke them. Then he gave them to the disciples to set before the people. They all ate and were satisfied, and the disciples picked up twelve basketfuls of broken pieces that were left over.

In this situation, Jesus met a particular need—a crowd of people was hungry. Jesus performed his miracles out of love and compassion for others. And the miracles were evidence that Jesus was the Messiah that John the Baptist predicted would soon arrive (Matthew 11:4-5).

Questioning Miracles

Many people refuse to believe in miracles because they feel that if God were allowed to intervene in nature, then there could be no scientific method. As Dr. Allan Bloom has written, "Scientists are to a man against creationism, recognizing rightly that, if there is anything to it, their science is wrong and useless…Either nature has a lawful order or it does not; either there can be miracles or there cannot. Scientists do not prove there are no miracles, they assume it; without this assumption there is no [naturalistic] science."[5]

Yet miracles do not necessarily contradict science. In other words, the fact that miracles occur is not a challenge to science. A miracle is a *break* from the normal laws of nature. That's what defines it as a miracle.

Dr. Gary Habermas of Liberty University said, in an interview, "If there is a Creator, a Designer of the universe, who has brought it into being, if such a being exists, then clearly he could intervene in the course of history and perform miraculous acts. It seems to me that we have to be open to *the possibility of miracles.*"

Habermas also notes that "most scholars, the vast majority today, would say that Jesus did at least the healing miracles and the exorcisms. Then they add, he did something *like* these but they weren't truly supernatural. So now the question is, What data do we have for the supernaturalness of Jesus' miracles? I'd say again, you're looking at a lot of reasons here that are very respectable."

Believing in Miracles

Even many skeptics of Christianity agree with the idea that Jesus performed miracles. Dr. Amy-Jill Levine, a professor of religion at Vanderbilt, suggested in an interview that "I do think Jesus was a miracle worker, along with several other miracle workers we have both in Jewish sources and in pagan sources. Would his miracle-working have been attributed to God? Certainly by some, but as we have even seen in the gospels, others would have said, 'Oh, yes, we agree he did miracles, but he does them by the power of Satan.' *The miracle working itself is unquestioned.*"

I (John) asked Dr. Craig Evans what has compelled so many non-Christian scholars to admit Jesus must have performed miracles. He responded, "I can remember, as a university student, the idea of any kind of a miracle story was laughed at. That has changed in the past thirty years. You can see it in popular culture. You can see it in the popular television program *Star Trek*. Mr. Spock wants to be a machine, right? He wants to be *scientific*. Science can solve everything. In the new version of it, you have a machine who wants to be a human! You have characters who want to be in touch with the inner spirit and channel and do all kinds of strange things. That show reflects the change that has taken place.

"In science, there's a recognition: 'Hey, we don't have a closed universe any more. We have to be open. We're not real sure about our origins any more. Maybe there is something beyond the physical universe. Maybe there *is* a God. Maybe miracles *do* occur.' That's a big change."

In a separate interview, Dr. N.T. Wright noted, "My history makes me say, 'Hey, put that stuff on hold for a moment,' just supposing Jesus of Nazareth really did rise from the dead. Don't start by saying, 'Did he walk on water?' Don't start by saying, 'Was he born of a virgin?' If you start with those questions, you go round and round in circles and you never get anywhere. Start by saying, 'How do you explain the rise of early Christianity?' If it comes back and says, 'It was Jesus' resurrection,' then you're going to have to hold your mind open to the fact that in the world, as Shakespeare said, 'There are more things in heaven and earth than are dreamed of in your philosophy.'"

New Testament scholar Dr. Darrell Bock agrees: "If you come to the text and you believe miracles can't happen, you kind of have a dilemma on your hands. You read these texts about Jesus multiplying the loaves or you read these texts about Jesus healing the blind, and you have to come up with some kind of explanation for what goes on. In fact, the healing of the blind is an interesting one because in the Old Testament, blind people didn't get healed. No one did that miracle. And that's not one you can very easily fake."

Every scholar I (John) have interviewed on the issue of miracles agreed on this matter. For instance, Dr. William Lane Craig remarked, "It would be bad methodology to simply dismiss [miracles] in advance before even looking at the evidence that they might have actually occurred. Otherwise, we could be ruling out the true hypothesis simply on the basis of a philosophical presupposition [a personal bias] for which we have no justification."

Outside Evidence for Miracles

Outside of the Bible, a growing amount of information has been gathered to show the reasonableness of miracles. Facts from psychiatry, medicine, and science are supplying evidence that may indicate miracles are happening in our world today. I (John) asked three researchers about these new findings, and I was surprised at the abundance of information that is showing support for the occurrence of miracles today.

Indicators from Psychiatry and Medicine

For example, Dr. Gary Habermas said, "I think another factor in favor of the miracles in the New Testament is that there is some very hard data I think that is difficult to explain away. I think of Marcus Borg, who reports in one of his books on Jesus that there was a team of psychiatrists recently who could not explain a couple of possession cases by normal scientific means. I also refer to a double-blind experiment involving almost 400 heart patients in San Francisco… they were monitored in 26 categories and those who were prayed for were statistically better in 21 out of 26 categories. Because the experiment was performed well, the results were published in a secular journal, *The Southern Journal of Medicine.*

"So, if you can see some of these things today, maybe you can't say, 'Oh, there's a miracle right there' but it makes you wonder a little bit. I have to say, can we be so quick to condemn the things Jesus did in the first century?"

Indicators from Science

Many scientists claim that all events must have some natural explanation or have a necessary cause. The supernaturalist makes a similar claim: *A miracle occurs whenever God deems it necessary.* If we had all the evidence (if we knew all that God knows), we could predict when God is going to intervene just as well as the scientist who can predict forthcoming natural events.

But even contemporary science is changing. Dr. William Lane Craig says, "It's interesting to note that in modern science—for example, in physics—scientists are quite willing to talk about realities which are quite literally metaphysical in nature…realities which are beyond our space and time dimensions; realities which we cannot directly perceive or know but which we may infer by certain signposts of transcendence in the universe to something beyond it.

"A growing number of scientists now believe that the evidence for the big bang theory points to a simultaneous beginning for all matter, energy, and even the space-time dimensions of the universe. This evidence has led them to place the cause of the universe independent of matter, energy, space and time. This evidence calls for the strong possibility of the existence of God."

Dr. Craig further notes, "If there is a Creator and Designer of the universe who has brought it into being, then clearly he could intervene in the course of history and perform miraculous acts. So in the absence of some sort of a proof of atheism, *it seems to me that we have to be open to the possibility of miracles.*

"To give an analogy, in the field of cosmology, the evidence indicates that the universe came into existence in a great explosion called the big bang at some point in the finite past. Many physicists are quite willing to say that this event required the existence of a transcendent creator and designer of the universe who brought it into being. Now, when we come to the life and ministry of Jesus of Nazareth, could it be that this same being has intervened in history in a dramatic and miraculous way as Jesus claimed? Shouldn't we be at least open to investigating those claims?"

Dr. Gary Habermas states, "To me, a naturalistic theory has to, by definition, fill in the blank. A naturalistic theory is not, 'You Christians are crazy! Things like this don't happen. I don't see miracles in my life and Jesus wasn't raised from the dead.' That's not a naturalistic theory. That's a denial." Many of those who argue against miracles simply deny them on the basis of their own predetermined biases.

Miracles also have purpose. God has a purpose and communicates something with each miracle. The miracles done through Moses confirmed that God had sent him and mocked the Egyptian gods whose domain the miracles overcame (Exodus 7:14–12:36).

Elijah didn't call down fire for nothing (1 Kings 18:16-40). The whole day had been spent by the prophets of Baal waiting for Baal to do something, but Elijah's God acted immediately, proving his reality and power.

Miracles do not contradict or destroy science. But trying to explain miracles by means of natural causes is definitely unscientific! Science actually points to miraculous causes for these events.

What's the Difference Between True and Counterfeit Miracles?

From a biblical perspective, Satan is not the same as God or even equal to God. In the beginning, God created everything good: the earth (Genesis 1:1), people (1:27-28), and angels (Colossians 1:15-16). One of the angels was named Lucifer (Isaiah 14:12), and he was very beautiful. But he was "lifted up with pride" (1 Timothy 3:6 KJV) and rebelled against God, saying, "I will make myself like the Most High" (Isaiah 14:14). In doing so, he also led many other angels to follow him, so that one-third of all the angels left their home with God (Revelation 12:4). These beings are now known as Satan and his angels (Revelation 12:7; see also Matthew 25:41). They have unusual powers and are said to be currently at "work in those who are disobedient" (Ephesians 2:2). Satan is able to disguise himself "as an angel of light" (2 Corinthians 11:14) and appear to be on God's side, but he does this with the intent to deceive. Satan is always working against God.

A Key Distinction

How can we tell whether it is Satan or God at work in a specific situation? The Bible gives us some tests so that we can know who is a true prophet and who isn't, and how to distinguish real miracles from counterfeit. Miracles are God-ordained supernatural interventions; counterfeits involve supernormal forces. The chart that follows summarizes the differences.

True Miracles	Counterfeit Miracles
under God's control	under Satan's control
supernatural power	a natural [mystical] power
associated with good	associated with evil
associated with biblical teaching	associated with unbiblical teaching
can overpower evil	cannot overpower good
affirms Jesus is God in the flesh	denies Jesus is God in the flesh
prophecies always come true	prophecies are sometimes false
never associated with occult practices	often associated with occult practices

One of the key distinctions between miracles and the occult is the use of spiritistic means to perform the acts. These are practices that claim to conjure powers from the spirit realm. In many cases they do just that, but the power is demonic, not divine. In the Bible, here are some of the practices directly linked to demonic power:

1. witchcraft (Deuteronomy 18:10)

2. fortune-telling (18:10)

3. communicating with spirits (18:11)

4. mediums (18:11)

5. divination (18:10)

6. astrology (Deuteronomy 4:19; Isaiah 47:13-15)

7. false teaching (1 Timothy 4:1; 1 John 4:1-2)

8. immorality (Ephesians 2:2-3)

9. belief in self as God (Genesis 3:5; Isaiah 14:13)

10. lying (John 8:44)

11. idolatry (1 Corinthians 10:19-20)

12. legalism and self-denial (Colossians 2:16-23; 1 Timothy 4:1-3)

Many of those who practice and teach pantheistic "miracles" not only admit that they use occult practices, but recommend them for others also. These characteristics show that such claims to miraculous powers are demonic.

Modern-Day Prophecy Claims

What about those who claim to be prophets today? According to the Bible, a prophet had to be 100 percent accurate (Deuteronomy 18:22). Yet today there are many who claim to have a "word from God" or a prophecy, yet it does not come true. The Israelites were told not to listen to prophets whose word did not come true. In fact, those who prophesied by any other god were to be put to death (Deuteronomy 18:20).

There are a lot of religions that seek validation by claims of miraculous deeds. For example, Islam's Muhammad is said to have moved a mountain, and Hindu gurus claim to levitate themselves and others. To make matters more complicated, there are also Christians making claims of miracles today. While some such claimants may be valid, others have been exposed as frauds. Even the loose way in which people use the word *miracle* adds to the confusion. For example, some say it's a miracle when a baby is born, and some say it's a miracle when they pass an exam at school.

How can you distinguish the truly miraculous from that which is not? Is it possible to define a miracle in such a way that false claims and merely unusual events are eliminated from the definition? Many Christians believe that miracles point to a God beyond the universe who intervenes in it. Morally, because God is good, his miracles always lift up his truth. Miracles help us discern true prophets from the false. True miracles are never performed for entertainment, but have the distinct purpose of glorifying God and directing attention to him.

The book of Acts presents many examples of miracle working, and a survey of them shows the contrast between good and evil miracle working:

- In Acts 3:11-16, when Peter healed a beggar, he attracted

attention. Peter then pointed everyone's attention to Jesus.

- In Acts 13:6-12 we read of a sorcerer who claimed to perform miracles yet opposed the apostle Paul's teachings about Jesus. His power was ended when Paul performed a miracle that made the sorcerer blind for a period of time. As a result, many people in that town believed in Jesus.

- In Acts 19:13-20, some non-Christian Jews attempted to perform an exorcism in the name of Jesus and were beaten by the man whom they were attempting to deliver. Many who heard about the encounter became Christians and publicly burned their books of incantations.

The Superiority of Biblical Miracles

Biblical miracles are clearly superior in stark contrast to dark spiritual powers. The magicians of Egypt tried to reproduce the miracles God did through Moses, and by means of illusions, had some success at first (Exodus 7:19ff; 8:6ff). But when God brought forth gnats from the dust, the sorcerers failed and exclaimed, "This is the finger of God" (Exodus 8:19). In the same way, Elijah silenced all claims of the prophets of Baal when he called down fire from heaven when they could not (1 Kings 18). Moses' authority was vindicated when Korah and his followers were swallowed up by the earth (Numbers 16). And Aaron was shown to be God's man for the priesthood when his rod budded (Numbers 17).

Finally, Christ also predicted his own death (Mark 8:31), the means of his death (Matthew 16:24), that he would be betrayed (26:21), and that he would rise from the dead on the third day (12:39-40). There is nothing like this anywhere in other religions. The resurrection of Jesus stands alone as a unique event in history. The physical resurrection of Jesus Christ from the dead stands as the ultimate miracle.

13

THE JESUS OF THE BIBLE:
Who Is He? What Can We Know About Him?

Jesus continues to make today's headlines. In recent years, much attention has been given to the supposed discovery of the Jesus tomb. There have been new archaeological discoveries that claim to reveal new facts about Jesus' early teachings. But how can we know what is *true* about Jesus? And more specifically, *what* can we know about Jesus from the accounts provided in the Bible?

The Bible says much about Jesus. But, there are seven key teachings about Jesus that make him and Christianity stand as distinctive from other world religions and their leaders:

1. Jesus is the prophesied Messiah whose birth and life were predicted hundreds of years in advance through very specific prophecies.

2. Jesus is unique in all creation; in all history and religion there has never been another like him.

3. Jesus was born of a virgin and is without sin.

4. Jesus is God and came to earth in human form.

5. Jesus is the world's one true Savior, who died on the cross for people's sins and offers eternal salvation as an entirely free gift.

6. Jesus physically rose from the dead as proof of his claims.

7. Jesus is the final judge. Someday he will return and judge every person who has ever lived.

In no other historical figure can we see the details of a person's life and nature predicted 400 to 1000 years before being born. The world has never known any other virgin-born and truly sinless person. No other man has ever claimed to be God and proved it through resurrection from the dead. These seven facts set Jesus apart as unique from all other people or religious leaders in human history. Let's look more closely at each of these facts, one by one.

1. Jesus Is the Prophesied Messiah

The Hebrew Scriptures are unique among the writings of the world's religions in that they contain scores of prophecies about a predicted future Messiah (as discussed earlier in this book). These prophecies extend over a period of 1000 years, and many are given in specific detail. The final prophecy was given 400 years before Christ was born. In our book *What's the Big Deal About Jesus?* we discuss over a dozen of these prophecies, at length, revealing that only Jesus Christ fulfilled them, and that he alone is the predicted Jewish Messiah.[1]

For example, Psalm 22 accurately describes a crucifixion—yet this description was given hundreds of years before the method of execution by crucifixion was invented and used throughout the Roman Empire. And this psalm was written 1000 years before Jesus was born. Jesus even quoted the first verse of this psalm while on the cross: "…they have pierced my hands and my feet. I can count all my bones; people stare and gloat over me. They divide my garments among them and cast lots for my clothing" (Psalm 22:16-18; compare with Matthew 27:35).

Isaiah 9:6-7 was written 700 years before Christ's birth. It speaks of the coming Messiah—a child to be born who will also be God and who will have an everlasting kingdom. In the Gospels, Jesus claimed he was God in human form and that he would have an everlasting kingdom (Matthew 16:28; 26:64; Luke 22:30; John 6:38-42,62; 8:42; 10:30,36-38; 18:36).

In Isaiah 53:4-12 is a prophecy that says the Messiah would be crushed and pierced for our transgressions, and that God would lay upon him the iniquity of all humanity. In the Gospels, Jesus claimed to fulfill this prophecy (Matthew 20:28; 26:28). In fact, Jesus repeatedly declared he was the predicted Messiah by continually stating he was fulfilling Old Testament prophecies: "You diligently study the Scriptures because you think that by them you possess eternal life. These are the Scriptures that testify about me" (John 5:39).

Micah 5:2, written 700 years before Christ's life on earth, called the Messiah eternal and a ruler over Israel. The passage also specified the exact location of his birth: Bethlehem. No one denies that Jesus Christ was born in Bethlehem and that he claimed to be Israel's true king (John 5:18; 8:58).

Daniel 9:24-27, which was written 500 years before Christ was born, prophesied the exact time at which Jesus would be put to death.[2]

Zechariah 12:10, also written 500 years before Christ's birth, prophesied that God would be pierced by the inhabitants of Jerusalem, who would mourn over him. The Hebrew text indicates Jesus would be pierced as with a spear, which is what happened (John 19:32-35). What is interesting about this Old Testament prophecy is that God, as Spirit (John 4:24), cannot be physically pierced. Thus, this prophecy must refer to an incarnation of God (God in human flesh).

Even for a person who does not believe in prophecies of the Old Testament, one fact is certain: The Septuagint, the Greek translation of the Hebrew Old Testament, was completed by 247 B.C. In other words, the Hebrew Bible was translated into Greek at least 250 years before Christ was born.

2. Jesus Is Unique in All Creation

The vast majority of people today have little understanding of how unique Jesus really is. Messianic prophecies are only a small part of Jesus' uniqueness. Even if you were to read the world's greatest religious and philosophical literature—the *Analects* of Confucius, the Qur'an of Islam, the *Vedas* of the Hindus, the teachings of the Buddha, or Taoism, or Shinto, or any of the great philosophers such as Plato or Socrates—these words pale in comparison to the words and deeds of Jesus.

In John 14:10, Jesus declares that his very words are the works of God. If Jesus really was God come to earth in human form, then this would be expected. Those who heard Jesus speak and act said, "You have the words of eternal life. We believe and know that you are the Holy One of God" (John 6:67-69).

- "The Jews were amazed and asked, 'How did this man get such learning without having studied?'" (John 7:15).

- "'No one ever spoke the way this man does,' the guards declared" (John 7:46).

- "He taught as one who had authority, and not as their teachers of the law" (Matthew 7:29).

The Bible also affirms Jesus' uniqueness in this way:

> God so loved the world that he gave his one and only Son, that whoever believes in him shall not perish but have eternal life. For God did not send his Son into the world to condemn the world, but to save the world through him. Whoever believes in him is not condemned, but whoever does not believe stands condemned already because he has not believed in the name of God's one and only Son (John 3:16-18).

The words translated "one and only" are translated from the Greek term *monogenes,* which literally means "one of a kind." This word emphasizes the unique nature of the person mentioned. In all human history there is no one else like Jesus—only Jesus is the literal Son of God. In John 5:18, where Jesus was even calling God his own Father, the Greek means God the Father exists "in a special relation to Jesus which excludes the same relationship to others."[3]

There are some other ways in which Jesus Christ is unique. For example, in *The World's Living Religions,* professor of the history of religions Robert Hume comments that there are three features of the Christian faith that "cannot be paralleled anywhere among the religions of the world."[4] These include the character of God as a loving heavenly Father, the character of the founder of Christianity as the Son of God, and the work of the Holy Spirit. Hume writes,

> All of the nine founders of religion, with the exception of Jesus Christ, are reported in their respective sacred scriptures as having passed through a preliminary period of uncertainty, or of searching for religious light. All the founders of the non-Christian religions evinced inconsistencies in their personal character; some of them altered their practical policies under change of circumstances. Jesus Christ alone is reported as having had a consistent God-consciousness, a consistent character himself, and a consistent program for his religion.[5]

3. Jesus Was Born of a Virgin and Is Without Sin

Many scoff at the claim that Jesus was born of a virgin. Yet his virgin birth is one of the most crucial beliefs of Christianity. In fact, if Jesus were *not* virgin born, there would be no Christianity. Why? If Jesus were not virgin born, then he was born just like every other person. This would indicate he was only human. If so, then his claim to be God was a lie.

In addition, if Christ were not born of a virgin, he could not have been the Savior of the world. As a man, he would have inherited a sinful nature from his parents. And if he were merely a man, he would have been a sinner and would not have been able to serve as a perfect sacrifice for the sins of the whole world (1 John 2:2). If Jesus were only human, his sacrifice on the cross would not have satisfied the justice of a holy God offended by human sin and evil. Only if Christ were both a sinless man *and* fully God could he properly serve as the atoning sacrifice for the world's sins. That is why the virgin birth of Christ is an absolute essential.

The Bible clearly teaches that Jesus was born of a virgin. In Isaiah 7:14, written 700 years before Christ was born, the Bible prophesies, "The Lord himself will give you a sign: The virgin will be with child and will give birth to a son, and will call him Immanuel." The name *Immanuel* means "God with us." When Matthew describes the birth of Christ, he declares that the prophecy in Isaiah 7:14 was fulfilled in Jesus: "All this took place to fulfill what the Lord had said through the prophet: 'The virgin [Greek, *parthenos*] will be with child and will give birth to a son, and they will call him Immanuel'—which means, 'God with us'" (Matthew 1:22-23). The Greek word *parthenos* has only one meaning: virgin.

Because Jesus was virgin born, he was able to be born without sin. He even challenged his own enemies to prove otherwise—"Can any of you prove me guilty of sin?" he asked (John 8:46). In John 7:18 Jesus said, "He who speaks on his own does so to gain honor for himself, but he who works for the honor of the one who sent him is a man of truth; there is nothing false about him." The apostles who lived with Jesus for three years were able to examine his life up close in critical detail. Their confession, echoed by many others, was that Jesus was sinless.

The apostle Peter said Jesus was "without blemish or defect" (1 Peter 1:19). The apostle John said, "In him is no sin" (1 John 3:5). Even the former skeptic, the apostle Paul, said Jesus "had no sin" (2 Corinthians 5:21). The author of Hebrews said that Jesus was "holy, blameless, pure, set apart from sinners" as well as "one who has been tempted in every way, just as we are—yet was without sin"

(Hebrews 7:26; 4:15). The Roman governor Pilate, after examining Jesus, said he could find no fault in him (John 18:38). Even Judas, who betrayed Jesus, confessed, "I have betrayed innocent blood" (Matthew 27:4).

To live without sin means to be *incapable* of lying or deceiving others. This means Jesus was incapable of committing or exhibiting any kind of unethical attitude or act. He could always, only proclaim the truth. If Jesus was indeed sinless, then logically, what he said about himself is true.

4. Jesus Is God and Came to Earth in Human Form

In what other religion or historical source do we find God living among his creation in human form? The closest resemblance can be found in Jainism, which claims, unconvincingly, an incarnation (from a polytheistic heaven) of its god and founder, Mahavira. However, Mahavira himself denied theism and condemned the practice of praying to or even having discussions about God. The only other religion with a concept of incarnation is Hinduism. But here the incarnations are of mythical gods, forever cyclical, and without ultimate meaning. According to the influential *advaita* school of Vedanta, the Hindu gods' incarnations are part of the illusions of the world and not redemptive in the way described by Jesus in the New Testament.

This is the gospel, the good news: that we *can* know God. If the incarnation is true, then people can know God. Jesus declared, "This is eternal life: that they may know you, the only true God, and Jesus Christ, whom you have sent" (John 17:3).

Adherents of other spiritual traditions often claim that their religious founders are unique, but their "proof" of uniqueness is lacking or found wanting. Yet Jesus clearly and uniquely proved that he was God in human form. The authors of the New Testament writings frequently stressed this unparalleled teaching. First, Jesus clearly claimed to be God. In John 10:30, he said, "I and the

Father are one." The word "one" in the Greek (*hen*), according to Greek authority A.T. Robertson, means not just one in the sense of agreement, but that Jesus was saying he and God are "one essence or nature."[6] Second, Jesus' claim to be God was understood by all people, including his enemies. Jesus said, "I have shown you many great miracles from the Father. For which of these do you stone me?" (John 10:32). His enemies said they wanted to stone him "because you, a mere man, claim to be God" (John 10:33).

In John 8:58, Jesus said, "Before Abraham was born, I am!" The Greek term here is *ego eimi*. Jesus was referring to Exodus 3:13-14, where God identified himself as the "I am." Jesus applied the unique divine name to himself, not only on this occasion but others. Jesus clearly claimed he was the God of the universe: "My Father is always at his work to this very day, and I, too, am working" (John 5:17). It was "for this reason the Jews tried all the harder to kill him; not only was he breaking the Sabbath, but he was even calling God his own Father, making himself equal with God" (verse 18).

5. Jesus Is the World's One True Savior

In contrast to the claims by people today that there are many paths to God, Christianity teaches that Jesus alone is the way. Why? First, because Jesus himself taught that: "I am the way and the truth and the life. No one comes to the Father except through me" (John 14:6). He also emphasized,

> I tell you the truth, I am the gate for the sheep. All who ever came before me were thieves and robbers, but the sheep did not listen to them. I am the gate; whoever enters through me will be saved. He will come in and go out, and find pasture. The thief comes only to steal and kill and destroy; I have come that they may have life, and have it to the full. I am the good shepherd. The good shepherd lays down his life for the sheep (John 10:7-11).

Second, Jesus proclaimed he was the perfect sacrifice for the world's sin. He said, "The Son of Man did not come to be served but to serve, and to give his life as a ransom for many" (Matthew 20:28), and "This is my blood of the covenant, which is poured out for many for the forgiveness of sins" (Matthew 26:28). Because Jesus is God's only Son, and because he was perfectly sinless, when he died on the cross for human sin, he became the only possible way of salvation for men and women. In other words, no one else is able to pay the penalty of divine justice against human sin. This is why the Bible teaches, "Salvation is found in no one else, for there is no other name under heaven given to men by which we must be saved" (Acts 4:12). Further, "This is good, and pleases God our Savior, who wants all men to be saved and to come to a knowledge of the truth. For there is one God and one mediator between God and men, the man Christ Jesus, who gave himself as a ransom for all men—the testimony given in its proper time" (1 Timothy 2:3-6). Perhaps this is why Jesus himself warned, "If you do not believe that I am the one I claim to be, you will indeed die in your sins" (John 8:24).

In addition, Christ offered a redemption unlike that offered by any other religion. Forgiveness of sins and eternal life are *freely* given without cost. Jesus said that he would personally raise all the dead and give eternal life to those who had believed on him:

> My Father's will is that everyone who looks to the Son and believes in him shall have eternal life, and *I will raise him up at the last day* (John 6:40, emphasis added).

> Just as the Father raises the dead and gives them life, *even so* the Son gives life to whom he is pleased to give it (John 5:21, emphasis added).

> I tell you the truth, whoever hears my word and believes him who sent me *has eternal life and will not be condemned;* he has crossed over *from death to life* (John 5:24, emphasis added).

> I tell you the truth, he who believes *has everlasting life* (John 6:47, emphasis added).

> This righteousness from God comes through faith in Jesus Christ to *all who believe.* There is no difference, for all have sinned and fall short of the glory of God, and are justified *freely by his grace* through redemption that came by Christ Jesus (Romans 3:22-24, emphasis added).

> He saved us, not because of righteous things we had done, but because of *his mercy* (Titus 3:5, emphasis added).

In human history, nothing similar has ever been proclaimed outside of biblical Christianity. As Martin Luther correctly noted, there are ultimately only two religions in the world—the religion of works and the religion of grace. Only biblical Christianity is a religion of grace because only biblical Christianity is a revelation from God.

Many people find it difficult to believe that among different world religions, Christ alone is the way to God, and that a person must believe in him for salvation if they are to receive eternal life. If Jesus was correct when he said, "All authority in heaven and on earth has been given to me" (Matthew 28:18), then no other option remains. It's not a matter of what we want to believe; it's a matter of what is true.

6. Jesus Physically Rose from the Dead as Proof of His Claims

If Jesus really did rise from the dead, then who can ignore him? But how do we know Jesus rose from the dead? On numerous occasions Jesus predicted his own crucifixion, down to the very day (Matthew 26:2). He also predicted his resurrection to occur three days later (Matthew 17:22-23; Mark 8:31; Luke 18:31-33; John 2:19,22). In fact, 24 prophecies about Jesus were fulfilled within the final 24 hours of Jesus' earthly life.

Prophecies Fulfilled in the Final 24 Hours of Jesus' Earthly Life

#	Prophecy	Prediction	Fulfillment
1	Betrayed by a friend	Psalm 55:12-14	Matthew 26:49-50
2	Money thrown to the potter	Zechariah 11:13	Matthew 27:5-7
3	Abandoned by his followers	Zechariah 13:7	Matthew 26:56
4	Accused by false witnesses	Psalm 35:11	Matthew 26:59-60
5	Beaten and spat upon	Isaiah 50:6	Matthew 27:30
6	Silent before his accusers	Isaiah 53:7	Matthew 27:12-14
7	Wounded and bruised	Isaiah 53:5	Matthew 27:26,29
8	Fell under the cross	Psalm 109:24	John 19:17
9	Hands and feet pierced	Psalm 22:16	Luke 23:33
10	Crucified with thieves	Isaiah 53:12	Mark 15:17-18
11	Prayed for those who killed him	Isaiah 53:12	Luke 23:34
12	People shook their heads	Psalm 109:25	Matthew 27:39
13	People ridiculed him	Psalm 22:8	Matthew 27:41-43
14	People astonished	Psalm 22:17	Luke 23:35
15	Clothes taken and lots cast for them	Psalm 22:18	John 19:23-24
16	Forsaken by God	Psalm 22:1	Matthew 27:46
17	Given gall and vinegar	Psalm 69:21	John 19:28-29
18	Committed himself to God	Psalm 31:5	Luke 23:46
19	Friends stood at a distance	Psalm 38:11	Luke 23:49
20	Bones not broken	Psalm 34:20	John 19:33,36
21	Heart broken	Psalm 22:14	John 19:34
22	Side pierced	Zechariah 12:10	John 19:34-37
23	Darkness over the land	Amos 8:9	Matthew 27:45
24	Buried in a rich man's tomb	Isaiah 53:9	Matthew 27:57-60

Even many critics agree Jesus was crucified and died at Roman hands and that the location of his tomb was public knowledge. Nor do many deny that a one- to two-ton stone was rolled over the face of the grave or that a trained military guard was set at the grave to prevent anyone from stealing the body. Critics even agree the tomb was found empty Sunday morning. But they offer different alternatives regarding what happened to his body.

Yet none of the theories from critics fit the facts. This is in large part due to the numerous resurrection appearances of Christ after his death. He appeared to many different people—to disciples who did not believe at first, to a crowd of 500, and to select individuals. He appeared to them in different ways, locations, and circumstances. These appearances eventually compelled belief, as the accounts reveal.

If Christ had died yet was physically seen alive by large numbers of credible eyewitnesses, then the Christian view of the resurrection is based on credible evidence. In fact, Christianity could not have come into existence apart from Christ's resurrection. The very existence of the Christian religion is, literally, historic proof of the resurrection. Without it, Christianity would be, as the apostle Paul wrote, in vain (1 Corinthians 15:12-14).

7. Jesus Is the Final Judge

No person can claim to determine the eternal destiny of his fellow creatures. But this is exactly what Jesus did. Because Jesus is God, and because he was the very one who died for the world's sin, he is also the one who will judge every man and woman who has ever lived and make the final determination regarding their destiny. The apostle John wrote:

> Just as the Father raises the dead and gives them life, even so the Son gives life to whom he is pleased to give it. Moreover, the Father judges no one, but has entrusted all judgment to the Son, that all may honor the Son just as they honor the Father. He who does not honor the Son does not honor the Father, who sent him.
>
> I tell you the truth, whoever hears my word and believes him who sent me has eternal life and will not be condemned; he has crossed over from death to life. I tell you the truth, a time is coming and has now come when the dead will hear the voice of the Son of God and those who hear will live.

For as the Father has life in himself, so he has granted the Son to have life in himself. And he has given him authority to judge because he is the Son of Man.

Do not be amazed at this, for a time is coming when all who are in their graves will hear his voice and come out—those who have done good will rise to live, and those who have done evil will rise to be condemned (John 5:21-29).

Jesus also taught:

When the Son of Man comes in his glory, and all the angels with him, he will sit on his throne in heavenly glory. All the nations will be gathered before him, and he will separate the people one from another as a shepherd separates the sheep from the goats. He will put the sheep on his right and the goats on his left.

Then the King will say to those on his right, "Come, you who are blessed by my Father; take your inheritance, the kingdom prepared for you since the creation of the world."

Then he will say to those on his left, "Depart from me, you who are cursed, into the eternal fire prepared for the devil and his angels."

Then they will go away to eternal punishment, but the righteous to eternal life (Matthew 25:31-34,41,46).

Jesus himself made it clear he will judge the entire world. The apostle Paul said that Christ Jesus "will judge the living and the dead" (2 Timothy 4:1). The apostle Peter said that God "commanded us to preach to the people and to testify that he [Jesus] is the one whom God appointed as judge of the living and the dead" (Acts 10:42). Indeed, God promises each of us that the *proof* of coming judgment can be found in Christ's resurrection. In other words, the future judgment is just as certain as Christ's own resurrection: "In the past God overlooked such ignorance, but now he commands all people everywhere to repent. For he has set a day when he will judge the world with justice by the man he has appointed. He has given proof of this to all men by raising him from the dead" (Acts 17:30-31). The Bible has warned everyone:

> We must pay more careful attention, therefore, to what we have heard, so that we do not drift away. For if the message spoken by angels was binding, and every violation and disobedience received its just punishment, how shall we escape if we ignore such a great salvation? This salvation, which was first announced by the Lord, was confirmed to us by those who heard him. God also testified to it by signs, wonders and various miracles, and gifts of the Holy Spirit distributed according to his will (Hebrews 2:1-4).

In light of this, perhaps non-Christians should reconsider the "win-win wager" of the brilliant Christian philosopher Blaise Pascal: If the Christian God does not exist, then because of Christianity's positive teachings, the Christian loses nothing by believing in God; but if God does exist and he believes, he gains everything in eternal life.

If God exists and a person rejects him, then the result is eternal hell. There will be nothing worse for the unbeliever if Christianity turns out to be true. As Jesus warned, "What good will it be for a man if he gains the whole world, yet forfeits his soul? Or what can a man give in exchange for his soul?" (Matthew 16:26).

According to the Bible, Jesus is God who has come in human form. He is completely unique and rose from the dead as proof of his claims. At death, each of us will face him as either Savior or Judge. It is not an issue of what anyone *thinks;* it is an issue of who Jesus *is.*

Those who are Christians must stand for the conviction that the Bible is God's Word for such claims to continue to hold weight among those who have yet to decide whether to follow Jesus. His claims are clear—and convicting. When we discover the evidence that points to the Bible as the supernatural, divine words of the living God, it fuels our desire to share the knowledge of God's Son, Jesus, with those who have yet to hear or yet to choose eternal life.

I f you've stayed with this book all the way to this point, you are likely someone passionately seeking truth, desiring to really understand what God's Word means in your life today. Perhaps your understanding has increased and your concern has intensified regarding the importance of learning about and living out the words of the Bible. You may be wondering, *How should I respond?*

To begin, we are all called to focus on the central character of the Bible—Jesus Christ. Three of the experts in this book shared with me (John) their concluding words about Jesus during one of our interviews together. To quote their words:

- *Dr. Craig Evans:* "If a person is going to say, 'Jesus is not going to be important in my life; I'm not going to believe in him,' then he's going to have to say that for reasons other than historical…the evidence is there, the sources are there, the picture is clear and coherent, and in my academic opinion, the picture is quite compelling."

- *Dr. N.T. Wright:* "Therefore, the historian, whether that historian be a secularist, a Muslim, a Christian, whatever— the historian has to ask, 'How do we explain the fact this movement spread like wildfire with Jesus as the Messiah, even though Jesus had been crucified?' The answer has to be, 'It can only be because he was raised from the dead.'"

- *Dr. William Lane Craig:* "The claim of the resurrection of Jesus alone makes him unique among the religious figures of the world. The fact that we have good evidence for it makes it more than unique. It makes it astonishing."[1]

Making a choice for Jesus is more than joining a religion; it involves entering a relationship. The process of choosing to follow Jesus includes some significant acknowledgments.

First, as sinners, our relationship with God is broken and we are unable to fix it. We may believe God exists, but he feels a million miles away, and we don't know why. The problem was well stated by the Jewish prophet Isaiah, who confessed generations ago, "All of us, like sheep, have strayed away. We have left God's paths to follow our own."[2]

Ever lied? Ever had an impure thought? Ever shouted an unkind word? We all have. God calls these unkind and hurtful actions *sin*. Our first step toward following Jesus is to acknowledge there is a God, and we're not him. We're the ones in need of a higher power; we are not a power within ourselves.

According to Scripture, our wrongful thoughts and actions hold severe consequences. Isaiah later said, "It's your sins that have cut you off from God."[3] Another Bible writer explained, "The soul who sins is the one who will die."[4] To be candid about it, Jesus said our sins, no matter how great or small, will result in eternal punishment in hell.[5] We don't like to talk about it, but that's the bad news in this story. We cannot afford to ignore that information, nor can we change it.

Yet the good news in this narrative is that the price to change our situation has already been paid. The cost? The cross. According to the prophets and apostles:

- "Yet the LORD laid on him the sins of us all."[6]
- "He was pierced for our rebellion, crushed for our sins. He was beaten so we could be whole. He was whipped so we could be healed."[7]

- "He bore the sins of many and interceded for rebels."[8]
- "Christ suffered for our sins once for all time. He never sinned, but he died for sinners to bring you safely home to God."[9]

Jesus said the primary reason he came into our world was to rescue us from divine judgment and provide a way for us to enjoy a close, personal relationship with him. He promised us we could have our wrongs fully and freely forgiven, our guilt removed, our joy restored.

To enjoy these benefits, we are called to accept the challenge to ask for forgiveness from our wrongs (an act of humility) and to trust in Jesus as God's only answer to our situation. How can we know this? From the most primitive times, the writers of God have communicated this truth:

> Seek the LORD while you can find him. Call on him now while he is near. Let the wicked change their ways and banish the very thought of doing wrong. Let them turn to the LORD that he may have mercy on them. Yes, turn to our God, for he will forgive generously.[10]

Jesus personally promised, "I tell you the truth, those who listen to my message and believe in God who sent me have eternal life. They will never be condemned for their sins, but they have already passed from death into life."[11] In a prayer to his Father the night before his crucifixion, Jesus shared, "This is the way to have eternal life—to know you, the only true God, and Jesus Christ, the one you sent to earth."[12]

The best part about this deal is that it's not based on the quality of our performance. Jesus certainly wants us to do what is right, but following him is based on his gift of grace. Our part is to take the step of faith and open this life-changing gift.

Paul, the great missionary and apostle, described this mystery, writing to early Christ-followers that "God saved you by his grace when you believed. And you can't take credit for this; it is a gift from God. Salvation is not a reward for the good things we have done, so none of us can boast about it."[13]

The big deal about Jesus is ultimately his great love for us. He has done all the work already. He invites us to embrace him in an intimate relationship for all eternity. Are you ready to join this spiritual revolution? Will you choose the way of Jesus?

There is no magic prayer to start the journey, but we'd like to offer a model to guide you. If you don't know where to begin, you can start with this:

> God, I ask your son Jesus to enter my life as my leader and rescuer. I know I've messed up. Please forgive me. I believe Jesus came back to life from the dead and place my faith in him for eternal life. I choose to follow Jesus from this moment forward. Please show me how to live for you.

If you have just made this request of Jesus, congratulations! Your life will never be the same. You will experience forgiveness, love, joy, and peace through all of life's ups and downs. And if you're coming back to begin afresh with Jesus, we want to encourage you in your spiritual journey as well. No matter where you've been, Jesus wants to help you move forward on an adventure of faith in close relationship with him. He promises to enter your life to give you a new purpose and passion.

We also invite you to let us know about any decision you have made or new growth you have experienced. Please email TakingAStand @johnankerberg.org with your story or write to us at:

The John Ankerberg Show
P.O. Box 8977
Chattanooga, TN 37414

We'll be thrilled to share Bible learning and spiritual growth resources with you. Allow us the privilege of partnering together with you to take a stand for the Bible!

Appendixes

The following transcript is an exclusive interview conducted by Dr. John Ankerberg with renowned scholar Dr. Norman Geisler. Dr. Geisler is the author or coauthor of nearly 70 books and hundreds of articles. He has taught at the university and graduate level for nearly 50 years and has spoken or debated in all 50 states and in 25 countries. He holds a Ph.D. in philosophy from Loyola in Chicago and is the cofounder and longtime dean of Southern Evangelical Seminary, in Charlotte, North Carolina.

The Bible: Who Wrote It?[1]

Ankerberg: Welcome. Is it really possible that the Bible is a book that conveys the very ideas and thoughts of Almighty God? Well, in this series of programs we're going to seriously examine the questions: Is the Bible really the Word of God, or nothing more than another collection of the words of men? If it is the Word of God, how do we know that this information came from God, and what was the process God used to get it to us? Some people say, "Some parts of the Bible came from God," but then add, "There are also a lot of errors in it." My guest today is philosopher and theologian Dr. Norman Geisler, dean of Southern Evangelical

Seminary. I asked him to start us off by answering the question, "Does it matter whether or not there are errors in the Bible?" Listen:

Geisler: Is it dangerous to live downstream from a cracked dam? Ask the people in Toccoa Falls, Georgia—a little college [town] nestled in the valley there, beautiful waterfalls. Behind it, a dam. The Army Corps of Engineers said, "The little hairline crack in the dam won't matter." One night, the dam burst and the waters swept down the valley and dozens of people were killed. It's dangerous to live downstream from a cracked dam.

What's the "cracked dam"? There are people telling us there are errors in the Bible–just small ones, not big ones–just little ones, just a crack in the dam. Are there errors in the Bible or is the Bible the inerrant Word of God?

Psalm 11:3 says, "If the foundations be destroyed, what can the righteous do?" (KJV).

Is the Bible the Word of God? Or is it the words of men? The Bible *claims* to be the Word of God and the Bible *proves* to be the Word of God. In this program we're going to show how this is the only book in the world that really claims to be, and proves to be, the Word of God.

Ankerberg: Now, there is no use thinking that the Bible came from God unless it specifically claims to be from God. Maybe you are not aware of the fact that there are not a whole lot of books that claim to be the Word of God to man. Obviously there are some, and we will talk about them later. We will see that just because a book claims to be the Word of God doesn't mean it is the Word of God. There must be evidence, there must be proof, that backs up such a claim. As we will see, the Bible supplies evidence that it did come from God. But right now: Does the Bible claim to be the Word of God? Does it say it just once or twice in a mysterious way? Or does it clearly, over and over, make this claim? Dr. Geisler tells us. Listen:

Geisler: First of all, the Bible claims to be the Word of God literally hundreds of times. It says, "Thus saith the LORD…" "The word of the LORD came to me…" Summarized very beautifully by two New Testament Scriptures—2 Timothy 3:16: "All scripture is given by inspiration of God" (KJV). Now, to be inspired means "to breathe into," not to breathe out. It's the Greek word *theopneustos.* All Scripture is breathed out of the very mouth of God. Matthew 4:4—"Man shall not live by bread alone, but by every word that proceedeth out of the mouth of God." David, on his deathbed, in 2 Samuel 23 said, "His word was in my tongue" (verse 2).

The Bible *claims* to be the Word of God. If the New Testament is Scripture and the Bible is said to be inspired Scripture, then the New Testament is also inspired Scripture, not just the Old Testament. So what is true of the Old Testament is also claimed in the New Testament. For example, Peter said in 2 Peter 3:16 that Paul's writings were inspired. In fact, in 1 Timothy 5:18 it quotes the Gospels as being inspired Scripture right alongside the Old Testament. So, it's not just referring to the Old Testament when it says "inspired," it's referring to the New Testament as well.

Ankerberg: Now, what do you think the apostle Peter and the Lord Jesus Christ himself thought about the Bible? Did they teach that the words in the Bible came from God? Listen:

Geisler: There's another important passage in 2 Peter 1:20-21. It says all the prophetic writings came as people were *moved* by the Holy Spirit. The word there is the same word [that's] used for a wind blowing on a sailboat moved along by the Holy Spirit. [The writings] did not come from the will of men, but from the will of God.

Now, all prophetic writings are inspired, and the New Testament is also a prophetic writing because it says it was written by apostles and prophets—Ephesians 2:20 and Ephesians 3:5. And even John was called a prophet in the book of Revelation, chapter 22, verse 18.

If all Scripture is prophetic and the New Testament is also prophetic, then the New Testament is inspired Scripture as well.

So we have literally hundreds of claims in the Bible, in addition to crucial verses, that tell us that the Bible claims to be the Word of God. In fact, let me mention one other thing. Jesus said that the Bible is the Word of God. He said in Matthew 5 that the Bible is imperishable—he said not a jot or tittle will pass away until all is fulfilled (verse 18). He said in John 10:35, "The scripture cannot be broken." It's literally unbreakable. He said it's exalted above all human tradition, in Matthew 15—"You have made the word of God void with your tradition," he said to the Pharisees (see verse 3). He said the Bible can be trusted when it talks about history, when it talks about origins, when it talks about science. He quoted Adam and Eve as being the first pair [of people] created by God. "Jesus said it, that settles it"—we used to sing the song in Sunday school. If Christ, the Son of God, said the Bible is the Word of God, then the Bible *must* be the Word of God, or else Christ is not the Son of God.

Ankerberg: So the Bible claims to be from God; the apostle Peter said the prophetic writings came as people were moved by the Holy Spirit, and Jesus Christ, the Son of God, said the Bible is the Word of God...Next, what about the New Testament? Dr. Geisler tells us.

Geisler: But what about the New Testament? Is it the inspired Word of God?...The New Testament is also the Word of God—Hebrews 4:12 talks about the Word of God being alive and powerful. Therefore, the New Testament is inspired as well. It's not just the Old Testament that claims to be the truth of God, but every book in the New Testament claims to come from an apostle or a prophet of God. So the entire Bible, Old and New Testaments, *claim* to be the Word of God.

Ankerberg: Now, from this evidence, I think you would agree that at least the Bible *claims* to be the Word of God. But because the Bible *claims* to be the Word of God, is that why Christians believe it? No. Dr. Geisler, [who] received his Ph.D. in philosophy…explains that Christians are not using the Bible to prove the Bible…

Geisler: Now let's remember, we're not using the Bible to prove the Bible here. We're simply saying, What does the Bible claim for itself? It's like asking me, "Who are you?" And I say, "My name is Norman Geisler. I live in Charlotte, North Carolina." You could verify whether that's true. We're simply asking, What does the Bible say about itself? What does the Bible claim? And the Bible claims in a short sentence or two to be the very written Word of God, from God, through men of God, to the people of God.

Now the question is, Is what the Bible claims to be true really true? What are the credentials for this claim?

Of course, any book can claim to be inspired. The Qur'an claims to be inspired. Muslims believe it's the very word of God. [The Hindus claim] the Bhagavad Gita…to be the inspired word of God. Mormons claim the Book of Mormon is the word of God. So we've got a lot of books out there saying, "I am the Word of God!" How do we know which one *is* the Word of God? What are the credentials, what are the evidences, for the Bible being the Word of God?

First of all, the Bible claims to be and proves to be the Word of God in a way that no other book in the world proves to be what it claims to be. The Bible is supernaturally confirmed. Miracles are acts of God to demonstrate that a prophet of God is telling the truth of God. For example, when Moses was called by God to go and talk to his people, Moses said, "They won't believe me!"

God said, "Stick your hand in your bosom. Pull it out." It was leprous.

"Put it back in your bosom. Pull it out." It was healed.

"Take your rod. Throw it on the ground." It became a serpent.

"Pick it up." It became a rod in his hand.

"Strike the water," and the water divided and the people walked across. In other words, [God] gave His prophets miracles to confirm who they were.

The same thing was true of Elijah in 1 Kings 18. Who is the true God, Yahweh or Baal?

Okay. Pray to Baal. If a fire comes down from heaven, then Baal is God.

It didn't come.

Okay, pray to Yahweh. Elijah prayed to Yahweh. Fire came down, consumed the sacrifice, licked up the water, and Elijah said, "Any more questions?"

In other words, God confirmed who his prophets were by miracles.

The same thing [happens] in the New Testament. Acts 2:22… Jesus [was] a man confirmed by signs and wonders. Even Nicodemus, who came to Jesus by night, said, "We know you are a teacher come from God because nobody can do the miracles that you do except God be with him" (see John 3:2).

Hebrews 2:3-4 [says God] confirmed [His Word] by signs and wonders.

This is the only book in the world that is confirmed by *acts* of God to *be* the Word of God.

Ankerberg: Now, we've seen that the Bible claims to be the Word of God, but some other religious books [make the same claim]. Let's compare the evidence the Bible offers as proof for being the unique Word of God with the Bhagavad Gita of the Hindus, the Qur'an of the Muslims, and the Book of Mormon of the Mormons. Listen:

Geisler: Let's take a look by comparison at some of these other books. Are there miracles in the Bhagavad Gita…saying that this is the word of God? There were no miracles. How about the Qur'an? As a matter of fact, in the Qur'an Muhammad refused to perform miracles. And the interesting thing is, they say Jesus performed miracles in the Qur'an, including resurrecting from the dead. They say

God used to perform miracles through his prophets to confirm that they were prophets. And then when Muhammad himself was asked, "Perform a miracle to prove that you're a prophet," he said, "Here, read this Sura, read this chapter of the Qur'an." In other words, he couldn't come forth with the credentials. He had the claim, but he had no credentials to prove it.

What about the Book of Mormon? The Mormons say that's the word of God. The problem is, the Bible tells us...you can test to see whether a prophet is telling the truth or not by whether he makes prophecies that are false—Deuteronomy chapter 18.

Joseph Smith predicted that the temple would be rebuilt in Zion, Missouri, and even gave the date for it. Didn't happen. False prophecy.

The Bible gives hundreds of predictions years in advance that are literally true, and I want to take a look at those in a little more detail.

The Bible claims to be the Word of God and the Bible proves to be the Word of God.

Number one, it proves to be because the authors of Scripture were confirmed by miracles. Moses, Elijah, Jesus, the New Testament writers, the apostle Paul.

Second, the Bible proves to be the Word of God by supernatural predictions made hundreds of years in advance. There is no other book in the world where there are literally hundreds of predictions made hundreds of years in advance, even by the dates that critics accept, that came literally true.

For example, the Bible predicted that Jesus would be born of a woman in Genesis 3:15; that he would come from the seed of Abraham (Genesis 12); that he would come from the tribe of Judah in Genesis 49; that he would come of the dynasty of David in 2 Samuel 7; that he would be born of a virgin (Isaiah 7:14); that he would be born in the city of Bethlehem in Micah 5:2; and that he would be crucified—get this—that he would be crucified and killed 483 years after 444 B.C.... Daniel said, in essence, "Four hundred and eighty-three years from the time of the command to build the temple, rebuild the city of Jerusalem, that the Messiah would be cut off" (see 9:25-26). That happened literally because between 444 B.C. and A.D. 33 it is literally 483 years.

You say, "Wait a minute. You must be on modern math. Much learning doth make thee mad."

No. Four hundred and forty-four plus 33 is 477. But these are lunar years of 360 days. Twelve times 30 is the Jewish calendar. You have to add five more days. So five days times 483 years is six more years and 477 and six is 483 exactly.

Now, show me any book in the world that predicted something that would happen hundreds of years in advance, what city, how, what year, what dynasty, what ethnic group. Jesus came and literally fulfilled all these predictions. This is a supernatural book.

Ankerberg: Now, in listening to what Dr. Geisler just said about fulfilled prophecy being proof that the Bible came from God, maybe you're wondering, *Are biblical prophecies the same as the psychic predictions being made in the tabloids at the supermarket?* The answer is no. Dr. Geisler explains the big difference. Listen:

Geisler: You've heard skeptics say, "Well, what's so great about that? Psychics make predictions, too." Well, they do. But the problem is, they're usually wrong. Several years ago they did a study of psychics' predictions for that year and found out they were 90 percent wrong. In fact, just a couple years ago, of all the specific predictions that were made by psychics, they were 100 percent wrong on that year.

Well, didn't Jeanne Dixon make great predictions about Kennedy's assassination?

Well, number one, she never mentioned Kennedy. And number two, she never mentioned the means of assassination. All she said was a Democrat would die in office.

And in a twenty-year cycle they had been doing that for the last hundred years or more, but what they don't tell you is that she, like the rest of the psychics, is wrong 80 to 90 percent of the time.

For example, she predicted that Jacqueline Kennedy would not remarry. She remarried the next day [after the prediction] Aristotle Onassis. Not a very good prediction.

Ankerberg: Well, this is just our first program in this series entitled, "Is the Bible Unique or Just Another Religious Book?" I asked Dr. Geisler to summarize why it is that we as Christians believe the Bible came from God, and to introduce next week's topic:

Geisler: So the Bible claims to be and the Bible proves to be the Word of God. It proves to be because the authors were supernaturally confirmed. It proves to be because there were supernatural predictions made hundreds of years in advance that literally came true. It also proves to be because the Bible has amazing unity. It was written by forty people over a period of fifteen hundred years in two different languages—Hebrew in the Old Testament; Greek in the New Testament—on hundreds of different topics. And yet, it has amazing unity. The same story from beginning to end. God created man; he fell. Christ was sent to save us. He's going to come back to defeat evil and bring in the eternal kingdom. No other book in the world written by forty authors over fifteen hundred years on a similar topic with hundreds of little subtopics would ever come out with this kind of unity.

For example, take a medical advisor. Suppose we had forty doctors over fifteen hundred years telling us the solution to sickness. One chapter would read, "It's all in demons." Another chapter would read, "Well, it's in the blood." The blood-letters from the barber pole, you know. Take the blood out. George Washington died probably from blood-letters.

Another chapter would say, "It's all in your mind."

[By contrast, the Bible has] unity. The Bible has the same problem, the same solution, with all this great diversity, this amazing unity. It shows there must be one Mind behind it using these authors to bring about these marvelous truths. The Bible claims to be and proves to be the Word of God by supernatural miracles, by amazing predictions, and by incredible unity.

I know the skeptic is saying, "Well, what about all those errors in the Bible?"

Let me say something. The Bible is the Word of God. The Word of God cannot err. Therefore, the Bible cannot err.

Appendix Two:
An Encouragement to Read the Bible

Have you ever read the Bible through from cover to cover? If not, why not start today?

- The Bible shares where we came from, and why
- The Bible reveals our purpose for life
- The Bible teaches us who God is
- The Bible explains how and why Jesus came to earth
- The Bible provides comfort for difficult times
- The Bible offers role models for us to follow
- The Bible provides us with guidelines for living God's way
- The Bible is God's love letter to us

Why not begin today and read through the entire Bible over the next year?

To help, we have compiled a reading guide online that you can print out to record your progress for each day. It can be found at www.johnankerberg.org under "The Daily Journey" or at http://www.johnankerberg.org/harbor2/daily/dailyindex.htm. This guide will take you through the Bible more or less chronologically. Each day you will read two or three chapters from the Old Testament and one chapter from the New Testament.

In addition, we have provided excerpts from the writings of classic and contemporary Christian writers such as Charles Spurgeon, James Boice, Matthew Henry, Walter Kaiser, Gleason Archer, and many others to help you understand what you are reading. It is our hope these thoughts will help you to see that "all Scripture is given by inspiration of God, and is profitable for doctrine, for reproof, for correction, for instruction in righteousness, that the man of God may be complete, thoroughly equipped for every good work" (2 Timothy 3:16-17 NKJV).

Enjoy each new day as you accept the challenge to learn about God through reading every verse of his Word over the next year. You can look forward to the changes he will make in your life as you grow in your understanding of biblical truth.

Additional Resources

nterested in learning more? We have listed below resources that are available from The Ankerberg Theological Research Institute, along with a list of helpful Web sites you may want to reference. **Please note** that the fact a Web site is listed here does not necessarily mean we agree with the entire contents of that site. These sites are listed because they are of a generally helpful nature.

Ankerberg Theological Research Institute Resources

The following Ankerberg resources can be ordered online at www.johnankerberg.org or by phone at (800) 805-3030.

Books

All the following books are authored or coauthored by Dr. John Ankerberg:

> *Defending Your Faith* (Chattanooga, TN: AMG, 2007).
>
> *The Facts on the Bible* (Eugene, OR: Harvest House, 2009).
>
> *Fast Facts on Defending Your Faith* (Eugene, OR: Harvest House, 2002).
>
> *Handbook of Biblical Evidences* (Eugene, OR: Harvest House, 2008).

How Do We Know the Bible Is God's Word? (Chattanooga, TN: AMG, 2008).

Knowing the Truth About the Reliability of the Bible (Eugene, OR: Harvest House, 1997).

Video Programs and Transcripts

The following topics are available in VHS and DVD formats. Most of the programs also have downloadable transcripts available.

Did Jesus Rise from the Dead? (Plus Q&A Session)

Did the Resurrection Really Happen?

Do Fulfilled Messianic Prophecies in the Old Testament Constitute Proof that God Exists and that Jesus is God's Messiah?

Four Historical Facts that Prove Jesus Really Rose from the Dead

From Skepticism to Belief—The Facts and Evidence that Can Lead You Step by Step to Belief in Christ

If Jesus Wasn't God, Then He Deserved an Oscar

Is Christianity Based on Fact or Fantasy?

Messianic Prophecies: Do They Point to Jesus or Somebody Else?

Refuting the New Controversial Theories About Jesus

The Claims of Jesus Christ

The Evidence for the Historical Jesus

The Search for Jesus Continues

Was Jesus Christ a Liar, a Lunatic, a Legend, or God?

What About the Missing Gospels and Lost Christianities?

What Proof Exists that Jesus Rose from the Dead?

Online Articles

Over 2500 online articles on Christianity and comparative religions are hosted on The Ankerberg Theological Research Institute Web site. For those dealing specifically with the evidence for the

reliability of the Bible and apologetics, see the link http://www
.johnankerberg.org/Articles/archives-ap.htm.

Helpful Web Sites

Here are some of the Web sites we have found helpful for studying about Jesus and Christianity:

- www.bible.org: Over 50,000 pages of Bible study material from some of today's leading Bible scholars.

- www.biblegateway.com: Search words and phrases from the Bible in multiple versions and languages with this leading resource from the International Bible Society.

- www.sermoncentral.com: Provides several sermon transcripts and notes for preachers and other teachers.

- www.leaderu.com: A ministry of Campus Crusade for Christ, LeaderU offers several links and articles on Christianity, ranging from entry level to academic.

- www.probe.org: A Christian media ministry that offers numerous online articles and audio resources on Christianity and culture.

- www.trueu.org: The college-aged outreach of Focus on the Family, providing several young adult-targeted articles on defending the faith.

NOTES

1. Citations taken from Frank S. Meade, *The Encyclopedia of Religious Quotations*; Rhoda Tripp, *The International Thesaurus of Quotations*; Ralph L. Woods, *The World Treasury of Religious Quotations*; Jonathan Green, Morrow's *International Dictionary of Contemporary Quotations*.

Chapter 1: The Uniqueness of the Bible

1. Benjamin Warfield, "Inspiration," from *The International Standard Bible Encyclopaedia*, edited by James Orr, vol. 3 (Chicago: Howard-Severance Co., 1915), pp. 1473-83, online edition at http://www.bible-researcher.com/warfield3.html.

2. From http://www.gotquestions.org/Bible-stats.html.

3. John Ankerberg and John Weldon, *Encyclopedia of Cults and New Religions* (Eugene, OR: Harvest House, 1999).

Chapter 2: The Inspiration of the Bible

1. Norman Geisler and William Nix, *A General Introduction to the Bible* (Chicago: Moody, 1978), p. 36.

2. Frederick Kenyon, *The Bible and Archaeology* (New York: Harper, 1940), p. 288-89.

3. Kurt Aland, *The Problem of the New Testament Canon* (London: Mowbray, 1962), p. 18.

4. Geisler and Nix, *A General Introduction to the Bible*, p. 134.

5. Norman Geisler, *Baker Encyclopedia of Christian Apologetics* (Grand Rapids: Baker, 1998), p. 93.

Chapter 3: The Reproduction of the Bible

1. Cited in the article by John Ankerberg, "If Jesus Wasn't God, Then He Deserved An Oscar," Part 3. Accessed at http://www.johnankerberg.org/Articles/apologetics/AP0701W3.htm.

2. This chart was adapted from four sources: 1) *Christian Apologetics,* by Norman Geisler (Grand Rapids: Baker Academic, 1988), p. 307; the article "Archaeology and History Attest to the Reliability of the Bible," by Richard M. Fales, in *The Evidence Bible,* compiled by Ray Comfort (Gainesville, FL: Bridge-Logos Publishers, 2001), p. 163; 3) *A Ready Defense,* by Josh McDowell (Nashville, TN: Nelson Reference, 1992), p. 45; and 4) the online article "Manuscript Evidence for Superior New Testament Reliability," by the Christian Apologetics and Research Ministry. Accessed at http://www.carm.org/evidence/textualevidence.htm#2.

Chapter 4: The Historical Credibility of the Bible

1. James W. Sire, *Why Should Anyone Believe Anything at All?* (Downers Grove, IL: Inter-Varsity, 1994), p. 221, citing Thomas C. Oden, *The Word of Life* (New York: Harper & Row, 1989), pp. 223-24.

2. Ibid.

3. Chauncey Sanders, *An Introduction to Research in English Literary History* (New York: Macmillan, 1952), p. 160.

4. Josh McDowell, *Evidence That Demands a Verdict* (San Bernardino, CA: Campus Crusade for Christ, 1979), pp. 39-52; and Norman Geisler, William Nix, *A General Introduction to the Bible* (Chicago: Moody Press, 1971), pp. 238, 357-67. Greek text figures are updated based on recently discovered Greek texts by the Center for the Study of New Testament Manuscripts at www.csntm.org.

5. McDowell, *Evidence That Demands a Verdict,* p. 42; Robert C. Newman, "Miracles and the Historicity of the Easter Week Narratives," in John Warwick Montgomery (ed.), *Evidence for Faith: Deciding the God Question* (Dallas: Probe, 1991), pp. 281-84.

6. McDowell, *Evidence That Demands a Verdict,* pp. 43-45; Clark Pinnock, *Biblical Revelation: The Foundation of Christian Theology* (Chicago: Moody Press, 1971), pp. 238-39, 365-66.

7. Newman, "Miracles and the Historicity of the Easter Week Narratives," p. 284.

8. William M. Ramsay, *The Bearing of Recent Discovery on the Trustworthiness of the New Testament* (Grand Rapids: Baker, 1959), p. 81; cf. William F. Ramsay, *Luke the Physician,* 177-79, 222 as given in F. F. Bruce, *The New Testament Documents: Are They Reliable?* (Downers Grove, IL: InterVarsity Press, 1971), pp. 90-91.

9. A.N. Sherwin-White, *Roman Society and Roman Law in the New Testament* (Oxford: Clarendon Press, 1965) from Norman L. Geisler, *Christian Apologetics* (Grand Rapids: Baker, 1976), p. 326.

10. Philip Schaff, Henry Wace, eds., *A Select Library of Nicene and Post-Nicene Fathers of the Christian Church,* 2d series, vol. 1, Eusebius: Church History, Book 3, Chapter 39, "The Writings of Papias" (Grand Rapids: Eerdmans, 1976), pp. 172-73, emphasis added.

11. Gary R. Habermas, *Ancient Evidence for the Life of Jesus* (Joplin, MO: College Press, 1996), pp. 66, 177.

12. Ibid., pp. 112-15.

13. Ibid., pp. 112-13.

14. C.A. Wilson, *Rocks, Relics and Biblical Reliability* (Grand Rapids: Zondervan, 1977), p. 120.

15. James Trimm, "Nazarenes, Qumran, and the Essenes," cited at http://www.essene.com/ History&Essenes/TrimmNazars.htm.

16. John Wenham, *Redating Matthew, Mark & Luke* (Downers Grove, IL: InterVarsity, 1992), pp. 115-19, 136, 183.

17. John A.T. Robinson, *Redating the New Testament* (Philadelphia: Westminster, 1976).

18. F.F. Bruce, "Are the New Testament Documents Still Reliable?," p. 33; cf. Craig Blomberg, *The Historical Reliability of the Gospels* (Downers Grove, IL: InterVarsity, 1987), pp. 247, 253.

19. Reprinted in *The Simon Greenleaf Law Review*, vol.1 (Orange, CA: The Faculty of the Simon Greenleaf School of Law, 1981-1982), pp. 15-74.

20. Irwin Linton, *A Lawyer Examines the Bible* (San Diego, CA: Creation Life Publishers, 1977), p. 45.

21. J.N.D. Anderson, *Christianity: The Witness of History* (Downers Grove, IL: InterVarsity, 1970), pp. 13-14.

Chapter 5: The Inerrancy of the Bible

1. Gleason Archer, "Alleged Errors and Discrepancies in the Original Manuscripts of the Bible" in Norman Geisler (ed.), *Inerrancy* (Grand Rapids: Zondervan, 1980), p. 59.

2. Paul Feinberg, "The Meaning of Inerrancy" in Geisler (ed.), *Inerrancy*, p. 294.

3. James M. Boice, *Does Inerrancy Matter?* (Wheaton, IL; Tyndale House Publishers, 1980), p. 15.

4. Charles Ryrie, *What You Should Know About Inerrancy* (Chicago: Moody Press, 1980), p. 30.

Chapter 6: The Prophecies of the Bible

1. J. Barton Payne, *Encyclopedia of Biblical Prophecy* (Grand Rapids: Baker, 1989), p. 13.

2. Ibid.

3. Peter Stoner, *Science Speaks: Scientific Proof of the Accuracy of Prophecy and the Bible* (Chicago: Moody Press, 1969), p. 4.

4. Ibid.

5. Ibid., p. 107.

6. Ibid., p. 109.

7. James Coppedge, *Evolution: Possible or Impossible?* (Grand Rapids: Zondervan, 1973), p. 120.

Chapter 7: The Context of the Bible

1. Gary Habermas, *The Historical Jesus* (Joplin, MO: College Press, 1996), p. 250.

2. Julius Africanus, *Extant Writings,* XVIII in the Ante-Nicene Fathers, eds. Alexander Roberts and James Donaldson (Grand Rapids: Eerdmans, 1973), vol. VI, p. 130.

3. Pliny, *Letters,* trans. Wiliam Melmoth, rev. W.M.L. Hutchinson (Cambridge, MA: Harvard University Press, 1935), vol. II, Book X: 96.

4. Moses Hadas, "Introduction" to *The Complete Works of Tacitus* (New York: Random House, 1942), pp. IX, XIII-XIV.

5. Ibid., 15.44.

6. Suetonius, *Claudius,* 25.

7. Suetonius, *Nero,* 16.

8. Lucian, The Death of Peregrine, 11-13, in *The Works of Lucian of Samosata,* trans. H.W. Fowler and F.G. Fowler, 4 vols. (Oxford: Clarendon, 1949), vol. 4.

9. The quotes of Galen can be viewed online at http://www.earlychristianwritings.com/galen.html.

10. The quotes and sources for these writers can be found online at http://www.rational christianity.net/jesus_extrabib.html.

11. See all the relevant excerpts from Celsus at http://www.bluffton.edu/~humanities/1/celsus.htm.

12. Cited at http://www.rationalchristianity.net/jesus_extrabib.html.

13. Craig Blomberg, in the interview "A Response to ABC's the Search for Jesus" on *The John Ankerberg Show,* 2001.

14. Complete citations of the church fathers in this section can be obtained at www.ankerberg.com/Articles/historical-Jesus/DaVinci/HJ-davinci-crash-davinci-code.htm#IS%20THE%20BIBLE%20AN%20UNRELIABLE%20DOCUMENT.

15. Colossians 4:12-13.

16. 1 Clement 36:1.

17. Ignatius, *Letter to the Ephesians,* 20:1.

Chapter 8: The Science of the Bible

1. Norman Geisler, *Baker Encyclopedia of Apologetics* (Grand Rapids: Baker Books, 1999), p. 692.

2. Hugh Ross, from his Web site at www.reasons.org/resources/apologetics/mysearch.html.

3. Mark Eastman and Chuck Missler, *The Creator Beyond Time and Space* (Costa Mesa, CA: The Word for Today, 1996), pp. 23, 84, 87.

4. See "101 Scientific Facts and Foreknowledge," at http://www.eternal-productions.org/101science.html.

5. Ralph O. Muncaster, *Examine the Evidence* (Eugene, OR: Harvest House, 2004), p. 165.

6. See "The God of Science," at http://www.bibletoday.com/archive/proof.htm.

7. Muncaster, *Examine the Evidence,* p. 161.

8. See "Scientific Facts in the Bible" at http://www.livingwaters.com/witnessingtool/scientificfactsintheBible.shtml.

9. For more on this topic, see "Advanced Scientific Knowledge" at http://www.bibleevidences.com/scientif.htm.

10. Muncaster, *Examine the Evidence,* p. 165.

11. John Ankerberg and John Weldon, *Fast Facts on Defending Your Faith* (Eugene, OR: Harvest House, 2002), pp. 92-94.

12. A special thanks to Ankerberg Theological Research Institute contributor Jim Virkler for his writing of this section. His science blog can be read at http://jasscience.blogspot .com.

13. Eastman and Missler, *The Creator Beyond Time and Space*, p. 156.

Chapter 9: The King James-Only Controversy

1. James R. White, *The King James Only Controversy* (Minneapolis, MN: Bethany House Publishers, 1995), pp. 22, 132-33.

2. Ibid., p. 133.

3. Ibid., p. 81.

4. As cited in Norman Geisler and William Nix, *A General Introduction to the Bible* (Chicago: Moody Press, 1971), p. 384.

5. Jack P. Lewis, *The English Bible from KJV to NIV: A History and Evaluation* (Grand Rapids: Baker Book House, 1984), p. 39.

6. In an interview on *The John Ankerberg Show,* from the transcript "Which English Translation of the Bible Is Best for Christians to Use Today?" p. 27.

7. Ibid., pp. 10-11.

8. White, *The King James Only Controversy,* pp. 224-28.

9. Ibid., p. 229.

10. Lewis, *The English Bible from KJV to NIV,* pp. 44-49.

11. White, *The King James Only Controversy,* pp. 231, 233.

12. Lewis, *The English Bible from KJV to NIV,* pp. 46-47.

Chapter 10: Answering Bart Ehrman

1. Cited from http://www.dallasnews.com/sharedcontent/dws/news/localnews/stories/ DN-biblesays_16rel.ART.State.Edition2.3e66907.html.

2. Gary Burge, "The Lapsed Evangelic Critic" in *Christianity Today,* June 2006, p. 24. Accessed online at www.christianitytoday.com/ct/2006/006/11.26.html.

3. From program two of "The Battle to Dethrone Jesus" on *The John Ankerberg Show,* 2007. The video, audio, and/or transcript of this program can be ordered at www .johnankerberg.org.

Chapter 11: The Culture of the Bible

1. The word *archaeology* is often also spelled *archeology.* Both forms are generally accepted. For an explanation for these differences, see the article at http://www.saa.org/public/ resources/twospellings.html.

2. E.M. Blaiklock, "Editor's Preface," *The New International Dictionary of Biblical Archaeology* (Grand Rapids: Zondervan, 1983), pp. vii-viii, emphasis added.

3. J.A. Thompson, *The Bible and Archaeology* (Grand Rapids: Eerdmans, 1975), p. 5.

4. Norman Geisler and Ron Brooks, *When Skeptics Ask: A Handbook on Christian Evidences* (Wheaton, IL: Victor, 1990), p. 200.

5. Clifford A. Wilson, *Rocks, Relics and Biblical Reliability* (Grand Rapids: Zondervan/ Richardson, TX: Probe, 1977), pp. 98-101.

6. J.A. Thompson, *The Bible and Archaeology* (Grand Rapids: Eerdmans, 1975), pp. 375, 405.

7. Cited in Geisler and Brooks, *When Skeptics Ask,* p. 202.

8. Wilson, *Rocks, Relics and Biblical Reliability,* pp. 112-13.

9. Merrill C. Tenney, "Historical Verities in the Gospel of Luke," in Roy B. Zuck, *Vital Apologetic Issues: Examining Reasons and Revelation in Biblical Perspective* (Grand Rapids: Kregel, 1995), p. 204.

10. John Warwick Montgomery, "The Jury Returns: A Juridicial Defense of Christianity" in John Warwick Montgomery, ed., *Evidence for Faith: Deciding the God Question* (Dallas: Probe/Word, 1991), p. 326.

11. Wilson, *Rocks, Relics and Biblical Reliability,* p. 120.

12. Cited in Geisler and Brooks, *When Skeptics Ask,* p. 179.

13. D.J. Wiseman, "Archeological Confirmations of the Old Testament" in Carl F. Henry, ed., *Revelation and the Bible* (Grand Rapids: Baker, 1958), pp. 301-02.

14. The following interview quotes in this chapter, unless otherwise noted, come from the program series "A Response to ABC's the Search for Jesus," on *The John Ankerberg Show,* 2001.

15. John McRay, *Archaeology & the New Testament* (Grand Rapids: Baker Book House, 2003), p. 156.

16. Eric Svendson, "Jesus' Infancy Outside of Matthew and Luke," *New Testament Research Ministries,* November 15, 2005. Accessed at http://ntrminblog.blogspot.com/2005/11/ jesus-infancy-outside-of-matthew-and_15.html.

17. Darrell Bock, in an interview on "A Response to ABC's the Search for Jesus" on *The John Ankerberg Show,* 2001.

18. D.S. Pfann, in an interview on, "Questions Surrounding Jesus' Birth," on *The John Ankerberg Show,* 2001.

19. D.S. Pfann, in an interview on "A Response to ABC's the Search for Jesus," on *The John Ankerberg Show,* 2001.

20. John 1:46.

21. Luke 1:26.

22. Matthew 2:23; 13:54; Luke 2:4,51; 4:16.

23. Magen Broshi, in an interview on "A Response to ABC's the Search for Jesus" on *The John Ankerberg Show,* 2001.

24. "Jacob's Well," accessed at http://www.christiananswers.net/dictionary/jacobswell. html.

25. John 4:29.

26. Further details can be found at http://www.allaboutarchaeology.org/synagogue-at -capernaum-faq.htm.

27. "Capernaum—Location Profile," accessed at http://www.ancientsandals.com/overviews/capernaum.htm.

28. Jean Gilman, "Jerusalem Burial Cave Reveals: Names, Testimonies of First Christians," *Jerusalem Christian Review,* Internet Edition, vol. 9, issue 2.

29. Rusty Russell, "The Pilate Inscription," accessed at http://www.bible-history.com/empires/pilate.html.

30. Ibid.

31. Darrell Bock, in an interview on "Questions Surrounding *The Passion of the Christ*" on *The John Ankerberg Show,* 2004.

32. Craig Evans, in an interview on "A Response to ABC's the Search for Jesus" on *The John Ankerberg Show,* 2001.

Chapter 12: The Miracles of the Bible

1. Thomas Huxley, *The Works of Thomas Huxley* (New York: Appleton, 1896), p. 153.

2. "Some Well-Known Miracles of Jesus," accessed online at http://www.bibleresource center.org/vsItemDisplay.dsp&objectID=F38BB037-BFF6-47FE-A828BEA35 B562AE8&method=display.

3. Benedict de Spinoza, *Tractatus Theologico-Politicus,* in *The Chief Works of Benedict de Spinoza,* trans. R.H.M. Elwes (London: George Bell & Sons, 1883), 1:83.

4. Interview quotes in this chapter are all from "A Response to ABC's the Search for Jesus" on *The John Ankerberg Show,* 2001.

5. Allan Bloom, *The Closing of the American Mind* (New York: Simon & Schuster, 1987), p. 182.

Chapter 13: The Jesus of the Bible

1. John Ankerberg and Dillon Burroughs, *What's the Big Deal About Jesus?* (Eugene, OR: Harvest House, 2007).

2. John Ankerberg and John Weldon, *The Case for Jesus the Messiah* (Chattanooga, TN: Ankerberg Theological Research Institute), pp. 66-72, 127-129.

3. Gerhard Kittel, ed., *Theological Dictionary of the New Testament,* vol. 4 (Grand Rapids, MI: Zondervan, 1978), pp. 740-41, q.v., "monogenes."

4. Robert E. Hume, *The World's Living Religions,* rev. ed. (New York: Charles Scribner's Sons, 1959), p. 203.

5. Ibid., pp. 285-86.

6. A.T. Robertson, *Word Pictures in the New Testament,* vol. 5 (Nashville, TN: n.p., 1932), p. 186.

Conclusion: What Should I Do with the Bible?

1. From "A Response to ABC's the Search for Jesus" on *The John Ankerberg Show,* 2001.

2. Isaiah 53:6 NLT.

3. Isaiah 59:2 NLT.

4. Ezekiel 18:4.

5. Matthew 25:31-46; John 5:21-29.

6. Isaiah 53:6 NLT.

7. Isaiah 53:5 NLT.

8. Isaiah 53:12 NLT.

9. 1 Peter 3:18 NLT.

10. Isaiah 55:6-7 NLT.

11. John 5:24 NLT.

12. John 17:3 NLT.

13. Ephesians 2:8-9 NLT.

Appendix One: The Bible—Who Wrote It?

1. The entire series of this transcript or DVD can be purchased at http://www.john ankerberg.org/catalog/BUR.html.

About the Authors

Dr. **John Ankerberg** is host of the award-winning television and radio program *The John Ankerberg Show*, seen in all 50 states and 200 countries. Author and coauthor of nearly 90 books, his research is used by universities and experts worldwide on world religions and the evidence for Christianity. He has three earned degrees: a Master of Arts in church history and the philosophy of Christian thought, a Master of Divinity from Trinity Evangelical Divinity School, and a Doctor of Ministry from Luther Rice Seminary. John lives with his wife, Darlene, and daughter, Michelle, in Chattanooga, Tennessee.

JohnAnkerberg.org

Dillon **Burroughs** is a staff writer for the *The John Ankerberg Show* and author or coauthor of 21 books, including *What Can Be Found in LOST?* and the revised Facts On series (with John Ankerberg and John Weldon). Dillon is a graduate of

Dallas Theological Seminary and lives with his wife and three children in Tennessee.

myspace.com/readdB   **readdB.com**

About the Ankerberg Theological Research Institute
Asking tough questions...offering real answers

Mission Statement

The Ankerberg Theological Research Institute (ATRI) is a Christian media organization designed to investigate and answer today's critical questions concerning issues of spirituality, popular culture, and comparative religions.

> *In your hearts set apart Christ as Lord. Always be prepared to give an answer to everyone who asks you to give the reason for the hope that you have. But do this with gentleness and respect, keeping a clear conscience, so that those who speak maliciously against your good behavior in Christ may be ashamed of their slander (1 Peter 3:15-16).*

ATRI utilizes five resources to accomplish this mission:

- *The John Ankerberg Show:* This award-winning weekly television program is broadcast into all 50 states and 200 countries worldwide via satellite. Its documentaries have also been featured as nationwide television specials.

- *ATRI Radio:* ATRI reaches thousands of people through its weekend one-hour program and its one-minute daily radio commentaries that air on nearly 700 outlets.

- *JohnAnkerberg.org:* ATRI's Web site reaches over 3.5 million unique visitors per year from 184 countries.

- *ATRI resources:* In addition to nearly 100 combined published books and three million books sold by ATRI authors in 16 languages, resources include over 2500 free online articles, audio, and video programs.

- *ATRI events:* Founder Dr. John Ankerberg has personally spoken to over one million people in dozens of countries spanning five continents.

Founder and president Dr. John Ankerberg is regularly quoted by media, including NBC, ABC, Daystar, and INSP. A board member for many Christian media organizations, Dr. Ankerberg also serves on the board of directors for the National Religious Broadcasters association.